SHAKE UP SCIENCE 4

Pearson Education Limited
Edinburgh Gate
Harlow
Essex CM20 2JE
England
and Associated Companies throughout the world.

www.pearsonelt.com

First published 2016
ISBN: 978-1-2921-4480-1
Set in ArtaStd, BemboInfantMTStd, BradleyHandITCStd, FuturaLTPro, GillSansInfantStd, ITCKabelStd, MemphisLTCYR, VAGRoundedLTPro, VAGRoundedStd, ZapfDingbatsStd, ZemkeHandITCStd

Acknowledgements
Picture credits
The publisher would like to thank the following for their kind permission to reproduce their photographs:

(Key: b-bottom; c-centre; l-left; r-right; t-top)

123RF.com: 4bl, 8bc, 30tr, 30bc, 38tr, 38br, 40, 46bc, 46br, 56/6, 66/2, 85t, Romanenko Alexey 38bl, Marian Bauer 26cr, Michal Bednarek 36, Kartouchken 8cr, Sergey Novikov 75b, Tomas Pavlasek 64tc, Mikhail Pelin 56/7, 87c, Nat Sukukawadee 28br; **Alamy Images:** Age Fotostock 26cl, Robert Harding 50t, Juice Images 66bl, Cal Vornberger 24t; **Fotolia.com:** abhijith3747 42l, ahavelaar 43/1, Anatol 41, brainsil 39 (d), 44b, decade3d 42r, Fefufoto 8cl, Mat Hayward 39 (c), 43/4, hkuchera 43/2, Iarcobasso 39 (e), Monticellllo 5t, Dmitry Naumov 39 (a), 45,

Niklas Ramberg 43/3, Rawpixel.com 9t, Olha Rohulya 44t, 82bc, RyszardStelmachowicz 46tl, Jonathan Stutz 58, Mariusz Szczygieł 5b, Gleb Tarassenko 32, treetstreet 20cr, Voyagerix 8b; **Getty Images:** Georgette Douwma 82c (bottom), Joe McBride 65, Martin C Parker 7b, James Randklev 14l, Stocktrek 51; **Imagestate Media:** Ian Cartwright 31/3; **Pearson Education Ltd:** Gareth Boden 69b, Malcolm Harris 12tl; **Shutterstock.com:** a_v_d 7 (a), alexskopje 27l, Scisetti Alfio 17bl, Andaman 28cr, Linda Armstrong 82b, Juan Camilo Bernal 52 (a), bezmaski 72br, bioraven 66/1, Max Blain 7 (e), Bluehand 21, Bonjo1013 52 (e), Stephen Bonk 37, 84b, Joggie Botma 79, 85br, Patrick Breig 82t, Brothwood 23tl, Vittorio Bruno 26tl, Volodymyr Burdiak 20bl, Roger Dale Calger 35cl, Leonello Calvetti 63c, 80t, 83tc, 85tc, ChameleonsEye 63l, 83tl, CreativeNature R.Zwerver 35c, daizuoxin 30br, Ethan Daniels 26br, 31/2, Michiel de Wit 23bl, 86bc (left), Denis and Yulia Pogostins 66br, Ian Doktor 56/5, EPG_EuroPhotoGraphics 75t, FineShine 26bl, fluidworkshop 57, Fotos593 50b, fotostory 46tr, Prochasson Frederic 52 (b), 54b, Tami Freed 52 (d), Fusebulb 43/6, Gardawind 31/5, gillmar 7 (b), gorillaimages 38tl, Michael C. Gray 38bc, Richard Griffin 17tc, 84tc, happydancing 48cl, holbox 66bc, Danny E Hooks 64tl, 87bc, Mau Horng 22tl, Inger Anne Hulbækdal 46tc, hwongcc 22br, Francesco R. Iacomino 52 (c), Iledic 69tr, Eric Isselee 23br, 24bc, 77, 86bc (right), 87b, Brian A Jackson 17tl, Jag_cz 14r, Jahina_Photography 48r, JeremyWhat 66r/4, junrong 13t, Sebastian Kaulitzki 42cl, 42cr, Cathy Keifer 16, Bill Kennedy 20cl, Kletr 7 (c), 38tc, 43/5, Kochneva Tetyana 30bl, 54t, Kokhanchikov 34t, 35b, Inozemtsev Konstantin 69tl, 80cl, Piotr Krzeslak 20tl, kurhan 72bl, Sergiy Kuzmin 7 (d), 28tl, James Laurie 22bl, 82c (top), Sergey Lavrentev 4bc, Lucky Business 74c, lunatic67 72bc, 80cr, Madlen 14cl, 28tr, Franco Mantegani 61t, Oleksiy Mark 66/3, Marques 31/6, MaxPhoto 61bl, Paul McKinnon 27r, Mark Medcalf 54tc, Christopher Meder 30tl, 33t, Dudarev Mikhail 8t, 86t, Tabby Mittins 31/1, Evgeny Murtola 46bl, n_eri 64tr, Maks Narodenko 64br, 85bc, Nic Neish 39 (b), Sergey Novikov 67, nulinukas 17br, Edu Oliveros 66l/4, Ollyy 66/5, orin 84bc, Pakhnyushcha 12br, 28bl, 82tc, Palo_ok 48l, Denis Pepin 35tl, Isabella Pfenninger 48cr, Photobank gallery 56/1,2,3,4, Photocreo / Michal Bednarek 33b, Mikhail Pogosov 74r, PRIMA 63r, 83tr, Roman Pyshchyk 86tc, ra3rn 4tl, 28c, Sergej Razvodovskij 7 (f), Reidl 24b, reptiles4all 26tr, 31/4, rickyd 4br, 7bc, Lincoln Rogers 12tr, Ron Rowan Photography 20tr, 22tr, Julian Rovagnati 72tr, Yuriy Rudyy 6, sakkmesterke 39 (f), samarttiw 30tc, sarka 12tc, schab 14cr, Umberto Shtanzman 64bl, Oksana Shufrych 4tr, sittitap 12bc, skynetphoto 26tc, smereka 35cr, Smileus 64bc, 83c, Solis Images 9b, Bernhard Staehli 52 (f), Wolfgang Staib 23tr, Alex Staroseltsev 69cr, Marek R. Swadzba

86b, Michael Taylor 54bc, 87t, teekaygee 35tr, Jeeranan Thongpan 17tr, Jeff Thrower 83b, Borislav Toskov 61br, 81t, Vacclav 52 (g), 87tc, Ronald van der Beek 69cl, 81b, Makarova Viktoria 74l, Pommeyrol Vincent 13b, Joao Virissimo 12bl, WDG Photo 72tl, 81c, Brian C. Weed 4tc, 84t, Matthijs Wetterauw 34b, withGod 35tc, You can more 11, Matej Ziak 20br; **Sozaijiten:** 72tc, 80b

All other images © Pearson Education

Cover photo © *Front:* **Fotolia.com:** Jonathan Stutz l; **Getty Images:** Gabriela Medina r; *Back:* **123RF.com:** c; **Fotolia.com:** Gleb Tarassenko l; **Shutterstock.com:** iunewind r

Contents

Unit 1 Technology and the Design Process

How can technology affect our lives?

1 What are the names of these machines? Unscramble the words.

1 nca rponee

can opener

2 cswer

____

3 eax

____

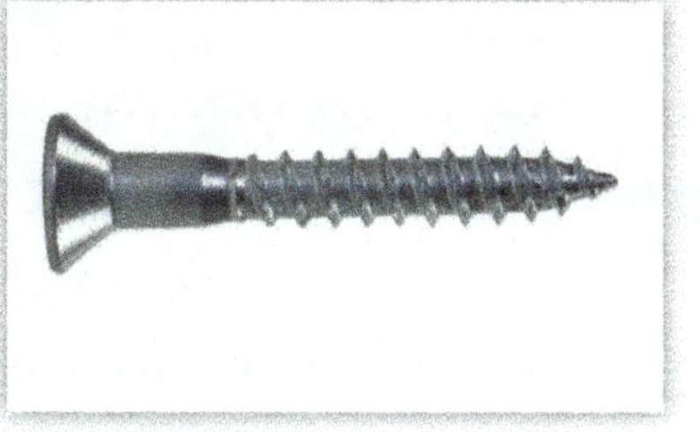

4 ocrsisss

____

5 sasewe

____

6 lehew

____

2 Which machine does what? Look at **1**. Match the machine to the job.

Which machine…

1 cuts paper? _____*scissors*_____

2 chops wood? ___________

3 helps drive a car? ___________

4 lifts someone up high? ___________

5 opens a can? ___________

6 holds two things together? ___________

3 **Where do these words go? Read the texts. Complete with words from the box.**

technology   wheels   complex   screw   design

Cool technology

Technology and (**1**) _____design_____ make sports better. When my mom was my age, she went roller skating. I go rollerblading. It's just like roller skating, only cooler! Rollerblades don't have four (**2**) _____________ like roller skates. They have a line of three to five wheels along the center, so they can go much faster! I love it!   *Becky, 11*

Do you ever think how (**3**) _____________ affects our lives? We use it every day in everything we do. Technology isn't only about (**4**) _____________ machines. It is about simple things, too. These things make our everyday life easier, but we never stop to think how great they are! Here's my example: When I skateboard, I get thirsty, so I have a metal thermos with a (**5**) _____________-top lid. I fill the thermos with cold juice and put it in my backpack. The juice doesn't spill, and it stays cold. How cool is that?   *Ed, 10*

4 **True or false? Look at 3. Circle *T* (true) or *F* (false).**

1 Becky's mom doesn't know how to skate.   T / **F**

2 Rollerblades always have four wheels.   T / F

3 Technology is complex machines only.   T / F

4 Ed says that technology makes our lives easier.   T / F

5 **How about you? Read what Ed says about his thermos in 3. Write about a simple thing that you use every day. How does it make your life easier?**

I use ____.

This is how it works: ____

It makes my life easier because _______________________________.

Lesson 1 · What is a machine?

1 **What is work? Circle the correct words.**

Work is the use of a **distance** / **force** to move an object across a **distance** / **force**.

2 **Are they work? Think of some activities that you do. Complete the lists with your ideas.**

Work	Not Work
kicking a ball	solving a math problem
__________________	__________________
__________________	__________________

Reading Tip

When you find a word in a text that you don't know, try to understand its meaning from the words around it. Even if you don't understand the word exactly, you can get a general idea.

3 **Machines we use. Read the text. Complete with words from the box.**

complex   design   machines   simple

Machines help us do things. The **(1)** ______________ process is a series of steps that we follow to design new and better **(2)** ______________. The objects in the photos in **4** are **(3)** ______________ machines. We call them that because they have only one or two parts. When we put two or more of these machines together we make a bigger machine. We call these **(4)** ______________ machines.

4 **What are the names of these simple machines? Match the words to the photos.**

1 inclined plane ___e___

2 lever ___

3 pulley ___

4 screw ___

5 wheel and axle ___

6 wedge ___

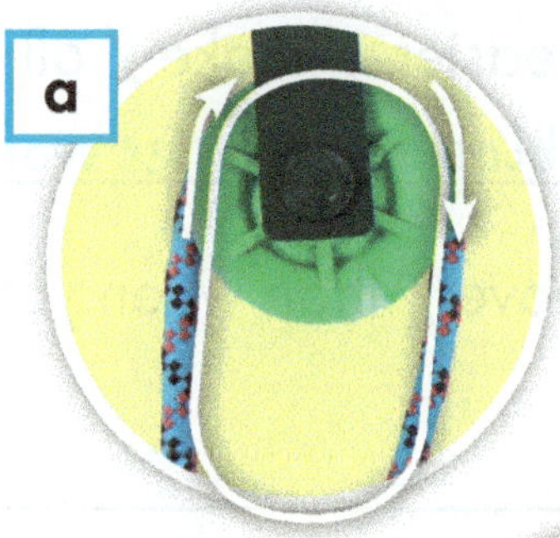

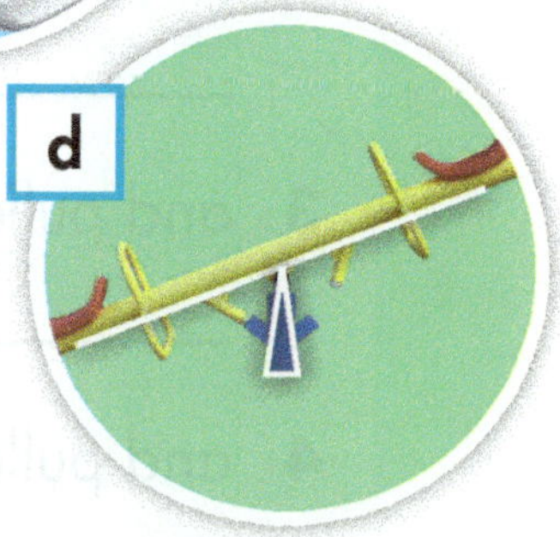

5 **Complex machines. Read the texts. Choose the best words to complete them.**

Steering Wheel

A steering wheel in a car is an example of a wheel and axle. When the driver (**1**) **turns** / **lifts** the steering wheel, this (**2**) **causes** / **creates** the axle to turn.

The axle (**3**) **makes** / **moves** the wheels of the car on the road. The driver doesn't have to use much force to turn the steering wheel, so it makes driving easier.

Crane

A crane uses a (**4**) **pulley** / **wedge** to lift things off the ground. Because it has a long (**5**) **lever** / **wheel**, it can lift big or heavy objects without using much force. A wheel and (**6**) **axle** / **inclined plane** help the driver to turn the crane and move things from one place to another.

6 **How do bicycles work? Put the phrases in order and make sentences about bicycles.**

1 bicycles / Like / work easier. / make / all machines,

Like all machines, bicycles make work easier.

2 are / a bicycle, / to move / than when you / With / on foot. / less force / you need

3 and pulleys. / in a / The simple / wheels, / levers, / machines / bicycle are

4 and pulleys / to move / your feet / the wheels. / The levers / help

5 to stop / help / More levers / the bicycle. / the brakes

7 **Can you recognize these simple and complex machines? Write what we do with them.**

1 doorstop = wedge → stop/door

A doorstop is a wedge. We use it to stop a door.

2 slide = ? → have fun

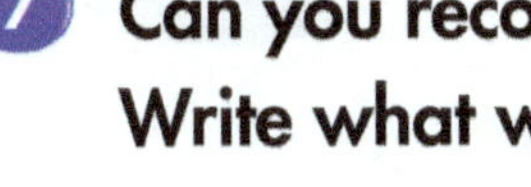

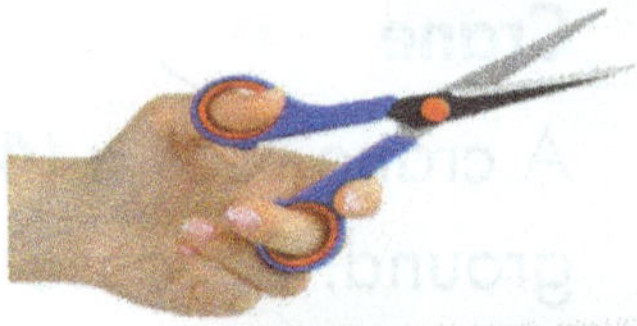

3 scissors = lever + ? → ?

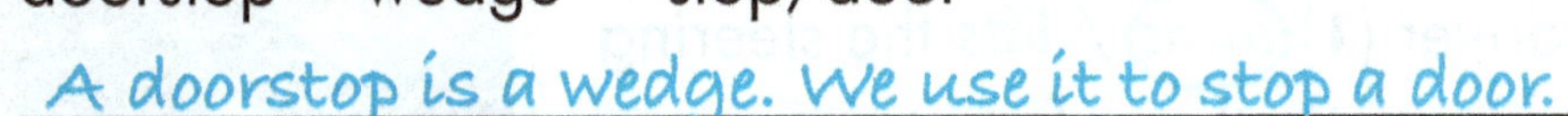

4 wheelbarrow = ? + ? + lever → carry/things

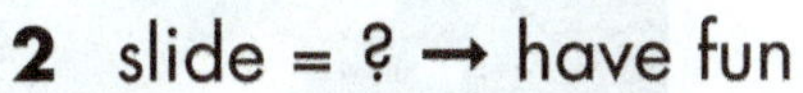

Lesson 2 · What is the design process?

1 What a product designer does. What machine did the product designer design?

____

Reporter: Adam, what is the difference between a product designer and a design engineer?

Designer: Let me show you. Look at this coffee maker. I designed it. My job was to make it look beautiful and easy to use. Katrina, the design engineer, took my designs and applied the technology that made it work. Together, we tested the prototype, we evaluated the results, and redesigned it.

Reporter: So, product design is more about art, and design engineering is more about technology.

Designer: That's a very good way to put it.

Reporter: This coffee maker came first in the design awards last year! How did that make you feel?

Designer: Very happy!

2 True or false? Read the statements. Circle *T* (true) or *F* (false).

1 A product designer and a design engineer don't do the same job. **T** / F

2 The designer wasn't interested in making the coffee maker easy to use. T / F

3 A product designer and a design engineer cannot work together. T / F

4 If you want a product to look good, you go to a design engineer. T / F

5 A design engineer tests how the prototype's technology works. T / F

6 Adam got an award for the coffee maker he designed. T / F

3 **What do these words mean? Match words from the box with the definitions.**

Prototype   Test   Evaluate   Redesign   Engineer   Design

1 ___Engineer___: his or her job is to design or build machines.

2 ___________: to make a drawing of something that will be made or built.

3 ___________: to use something to see if it works correctly.

4 ___________: the first working product of a machine that is used to test the design.

5 ___________: to say how well something works.

6 ___________: to make changes to the design of a product, to make it work better.

4 **Which stage goes where? Read what Adam, the designer, said later in the interview. Match each stage of the design process with a heading in the box.**

Identify the Problem   Test the Prototype
Design and Construct a Prototype   Communicate Results
Develop Possible Solutions   Carry Out Research

1 ___Identify the Problem___

There are no coffee makers that tell you when the coffee is not good to drink any more.

2 ___________

We looked for any technology that would help us.

3 ___________

We thought of a number of different things we could do.

4 ___________

When the designs were ready, we used them to build the first working model.

5 ___________

We made 342 cups of coffee with different types of coffee beans.

6 ___________

We met with the investors and showed them our results.

5 **Can you recognize these verbs? Write the past tense.**

1 design   _designed_

2 is   __________   3 test   __________

4 take   __________   5 evaluate __________

6 apply   __________   7 redesign __________

8 make   __________   9 come __________

6 **Machines and everyday life. Choose a verb from the box and complete the text. Choose the correct form.**

change / changed   buy / bought   listen / listened   play / played
have / had   need / needed

Which machine can you not live without?

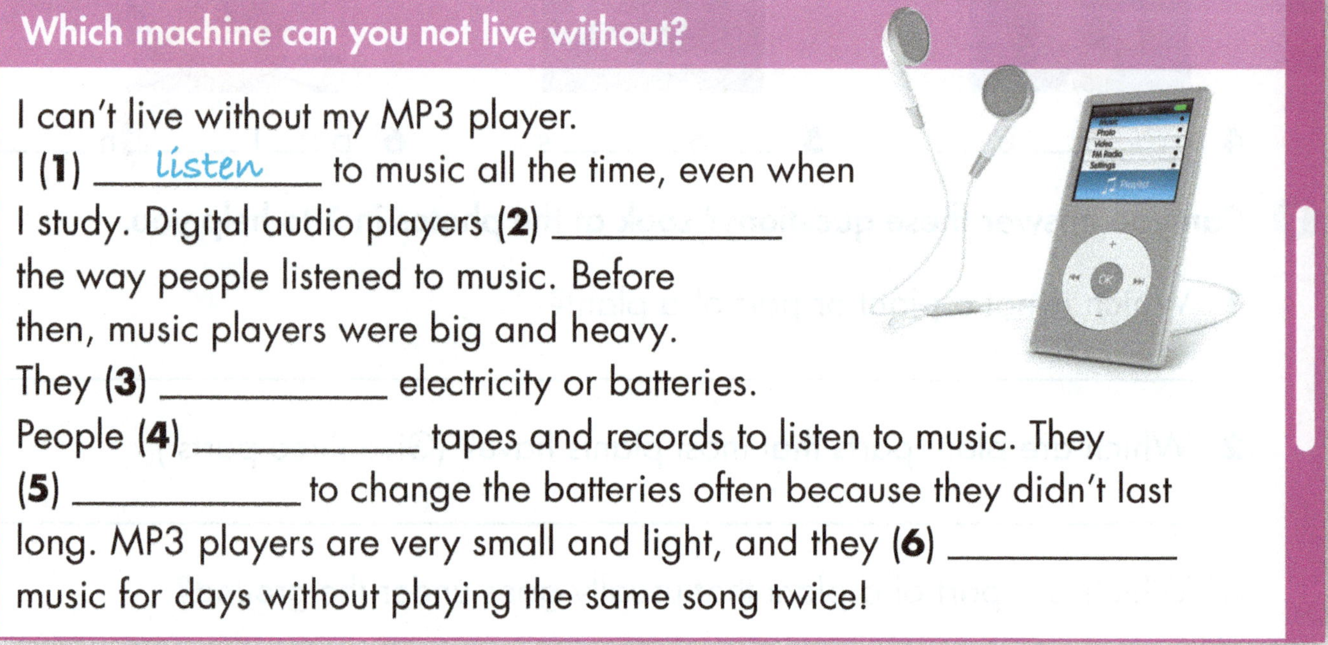

I can't live without my MP3 player.
I **(1)** ___listen___ to music all the time, even when
I study. Digital audio players **(2)** ____________
the way people listened to music. Before
then, music players were big and heavy.
They **(3)** ____________ electricity or batteries.
People **(4)** ____________ tapes and records to listen to music. They
(5) ____________ to change the batteries often because they didn't last
long. MP3 players are very small and light, and they **(6)** ____________
music for days without playing the same song twice!

7 **How about you? Write about a machine you can't live without. Say why you chose it and how it changed people's lives when it became available.**

____

____

____

Unit 2 Plants

How do plants change and grow?

1 Can you recognize these words related to plants? Write the missing letters.

1 s t e m

2 __ e e __ __ __

3 p __ __ e __ o n __

4 c __ c __ u __

5 __ o __ s

6 p __ l __ __ n __ __ i __ n

2 Can you answer these questions? Look at the photos in 1 to help you.

1 Which is <u>not</u> a plant or part of a plant?

____

2 Which are plant parts that most plants have? (Give three parts.)

____

3 Which is a part of a plant that usually goes under the ground?

____

4 Which is a type of plant?

____

3 **What helps a plant grow? Mark (✓) the things that help a plant grow. Then read the text in 4 to check.**

- [ ] sun
- [ ] air
- [ ] dark
- [ ] snow
- [ ] rain
- [ ] warm weather
- [ ] very hot weather

4 **What do you think the text is about? Use the title and photos to help you.**

____

It's a hard life—even for plants!

Plants need water, light, and the right temperature to grow. They usually don't grow well when it's too hot, too cold, or when they do not have enough light and air. But, some plants can grow in very difficult conditions.

One example is the cactus. It can grow in very hot places where there is very little water. When it rains, the cactus stores water to help it stay alive when it is dry.

Alpine plants live near the tops of very high mountains, like the Alps in Western Europe. The temperatures there are very low, and there is snow for a large part of the year. These small plants can stay alive under the snow.

At the bottom of the oceans, there is no air, and there is very little light. The water is very cold, and conditions are too difficult for most plants to grow and for most animals to live. But, where there is even a little light, there are tiny plants that grow in the water. These plants provide food for the creatures that live in the deep ocean.

5 **How about you? What's the name of your favorite plant? Where does it grow? Why do you like it? Write about it here.**

____

____

____

Lesson 1 · How do plants use roots and stems to grow?

1 What can you see? Match the different types of plant stems and roots 1–5 with the photos a–d.

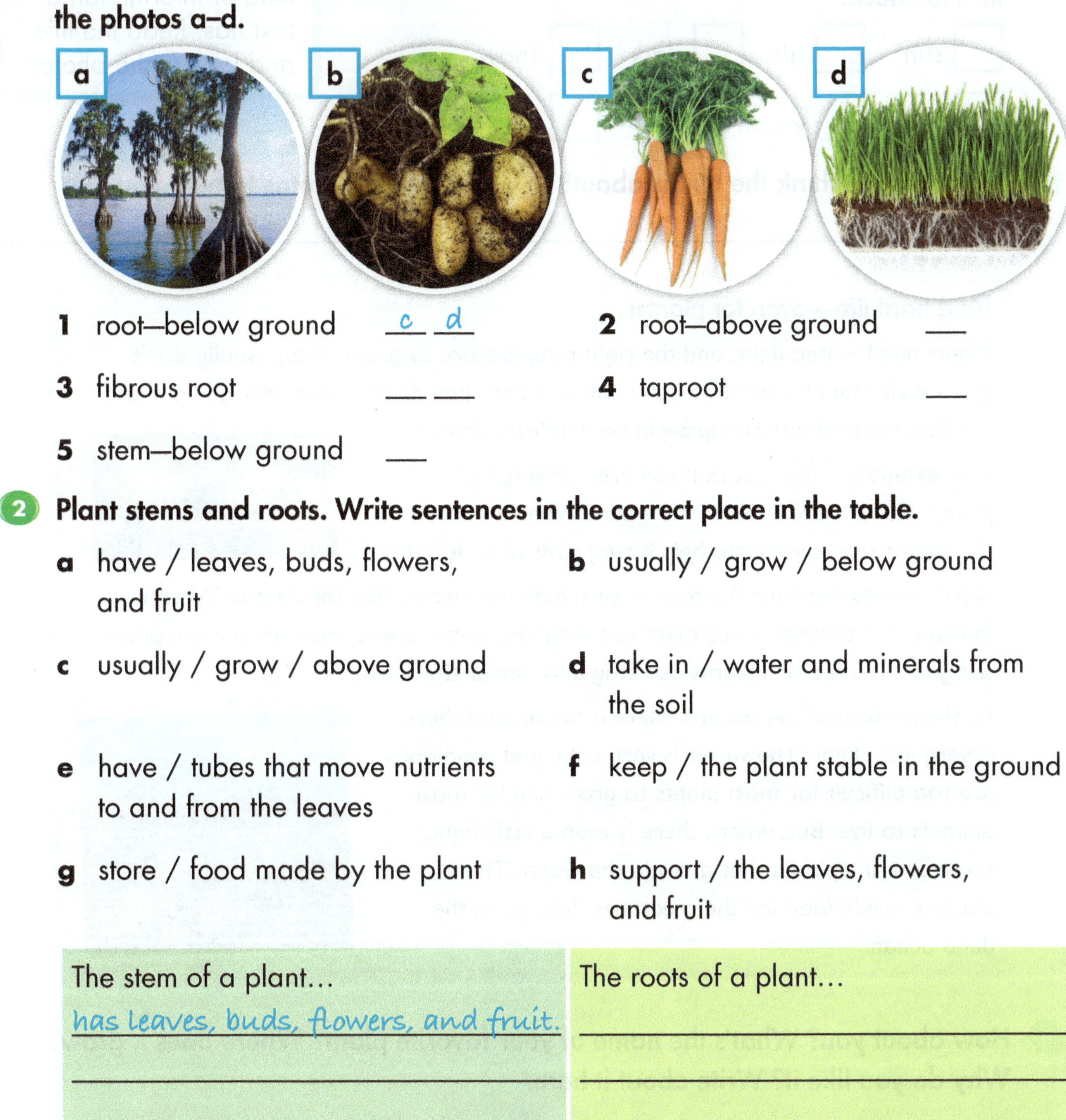

1 root—below ground ___c___ ___d___

2 root—above ground ___

3 fibrous root ___ ___

4 taproot ___

5 stem—below ground ___

2 Plant stems and roots. Write sentences in the correct place in the table.

a have / leaves, buds, flowers, and fruit

b usually / grow / below ground

c usually / grow / above ground

d take in / water and minerals from the soil

e have / tubes that move nutrients to and from the leaves

f keep / the plant stable in the ground

g store / food made by the plant

h support / the leaves, flowers, and fruit

The stem of a plant…	The roots of a plant…
has leaves, buds, flowers, and fruit.	

3 Do you remember that plants store water in their stems? Where else do you think plants store water? Read the text in **4** to find out.

____

4 Plants and growth. Complete the text with words from the box.

soil   nutrients   minerals   water   keep   store   take in

How do plants help people grow?

The roots of plants keep them stable in the ground. They also **(1)** _____keep_____ them alive. Plants need **(2)** _____________ to grow and be healthy. Their roots **(3)** _____________ all the nutrients they need from the soil. Some of these nutrients, like **(4)** _____________, are important for our health, too. We cannot eat the soil, so we eat plants. When we eat fruits and vegetables, we also eat the nutrients they have.

Plants use their roots to take in water from the **(5)** _____________. Plants **(6)** _____________ this water in their stems, roots, and fruits. We need water to stay alive, too. We can take water from the foods we eat. Did you know that carrots and apples are more than 80% **(7)** _____________? We still need to drink a lot of water to stay healthy, but fruits and vegetables are a tasty change!

5 Can you answer these questions? Look at the text in **4** again to help you.

1 How do plants get their food? _____________________________

2 Where do people get minerals from? _____________________________

3 Can we stay alive with only the water we get from food? _____________

4 Which other fruits and vegetables have a lot of water? _____________

6 How many fruits and vegetables do you eat every day? How much water do you drink?

I eat ____.

I drink ____.

7 Some plants eat insects—true or false? Read the text in **8** to check your answer. _______________

8 An unusual plant. Read the text. Complete with *from, to, up,* and *along.*

The Venus flytrap is different (**1**) _____*from*_____ other plants. No, it's not because it looks strange (well, it does), but because it eats insects! We know that plants take in nutrients (**2**) _____________ the soil. This plant comes (**3**) _____________ North and South Carolina. It grows in areas where the soil is poor in nutrients. This is why it eats insects for food. This is how it does it. The Venus flytrap has tiny hairs (**4**) _____________ the edges of its leaves. When an insect touches these hairs, the leaves close and catch the insect.

You can grow a Venus flytrap at home. You can buy one online, and they send it (**5**) _____________ your house. The Venus flytrap loves the sun and grows (**6**) _____________ toward the light. You need to make sure it gets plenty of sunlight.

9 What makes a Venus flytrap happy? Use this information to write sentences about keeping a Venus flytrap at home.

Soil: use soil that is poor in minerals

Water: keep roots wet

Light: put it in the sun (2 to 4 hours a day)

Temperature: keep it warm

Food: feed it two insects a month

A Venus flytrap likes soil that is poor in minerals. Make sure...

____

____

____

Lesson 2 · How do plants use flowers and cones to reproduce?

1 Can you remember what these are called? Label the photos with words from the box.

pollen cone   pollen   seed cone   seeds with parachutes   germinating seed

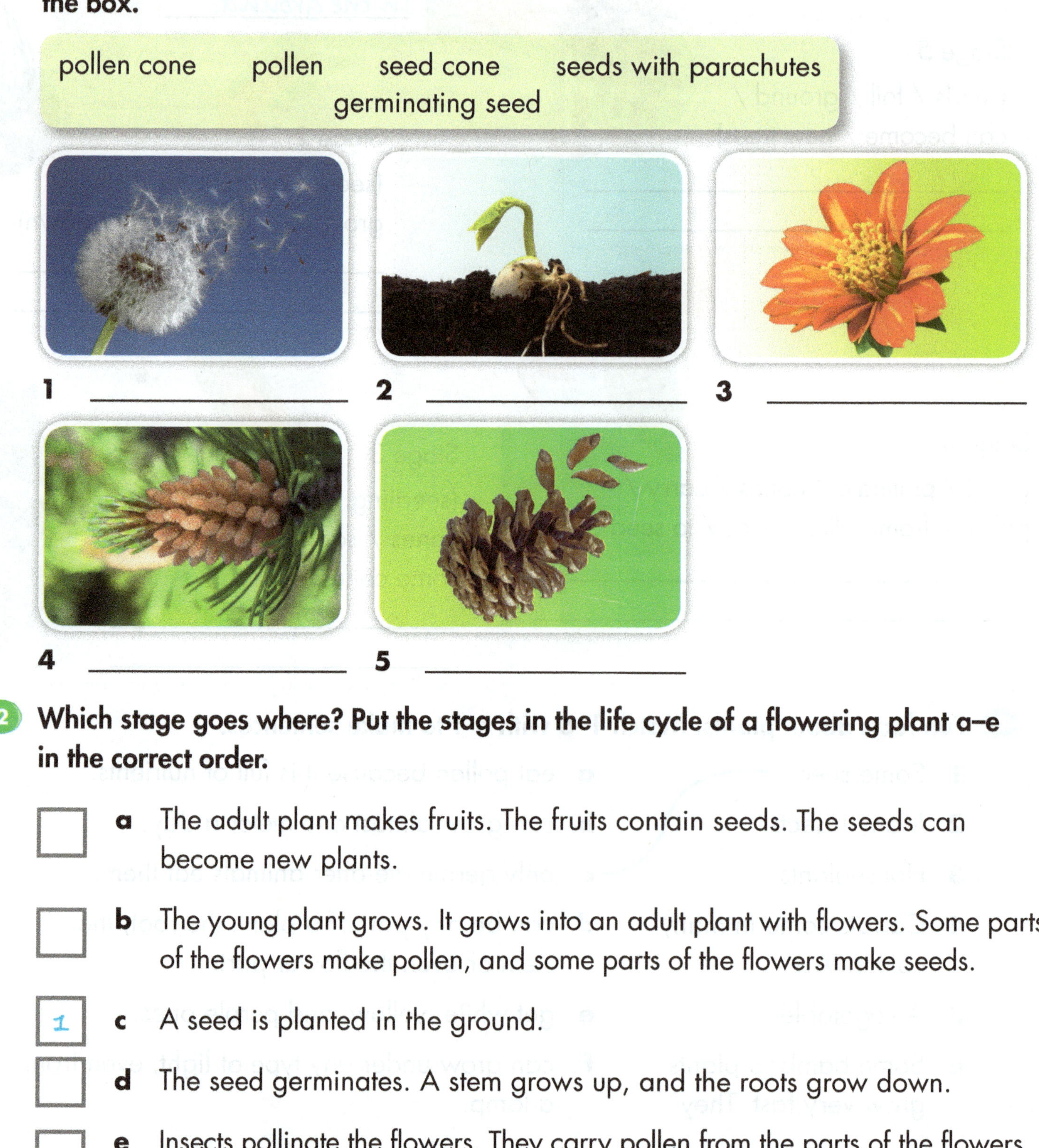

1 _______________   2 _______________   3 _______________

4 _______________   5 _______________

2 Which stage goes where? Put the stages in the life cycle of a flowering plant a–e in the correct order.

- [ ] **a** The adult plant makes fruits. The fruits contain seeds. The seeds can become new plants.

- [ ] **b** The young plant grows. It grows into an adult plant with flowers. Some parts of the flowers make pollen, and some parts of the flowers make seeds.

- [1] **c** A seed is planted in the ground.

- [ ] **d** The seed germinates. A stem grows up, and the roots grow down.

- [ ] **e** Insects pollinate the flowers. They carry pollen from the parts of the flowers that make pollen to the parts of the flowers that make seeds.

3 The life cycle of a conifer plant.
Write, using the words given.

Stage 1

A seed is planted in the ground.

Stage 2
(seed / germinates / stem / grow up / roots / grow down)

Stage 3
(seedling / grow / adult tree / cones / some cones / pollen / some cones / seeds)

Stage 4
(wind / pollinate / cones / carry / pollen / from pollen cones / to seed cones)

Stage 5
(seeds / fall / ground / can become / new trees)

4 Fun facts about plants. Match 1–6 with a–f to make sentences.

1 Some seeds
2 Many insects
3 Houseplants
4 Carrots come in many colors. We
5 A vegetable
6 Some bamboo plants grow very fast. They

a eat pollen because it is full of nutrients.
b can grow almost one meter a day.
c only germinate after animals eat them.
d can be any part of a plant: the root, the stem or even the flower part.
e get white, yellow, and purple ones.
f can grow under any type of light, even from a lamp.

5 **Plant reproduction. Complete the sentences with *some*, *any*, and *many*.**

1 ___Some___ plants can grow new plants from their stems or roots.

2 ___________ insect that carries pollen can pollinate a flower.

3 There aren't ___________ plants in the desert.

4 ___________ flower parts can make seeds. Other flower parts carry pollen.

5 ___________ seed can produce a new plant if the conditions are right.

6 Flowers come in ___________ different shapes, sizes, and colors.

> **Grammar Tip**
>
> **Some** plants live for a very short time.
> **Many** trees live longer than humans do.
> **Any** plant that has cones is called a conifer plant.

6 **Can you solve these plant problems? Use the words in parentheses and/or your own words to write your solutions.**

1 You want to buy a houseplant for your aunt, but she is often away from home. What kind of plant is best?

(*a plant that doesn't need…*)

A plant that doesn't need much water is best.

A ___________ is a good idea.

2 You have a potted plant that doesn't look very happy. What do you need to check?

(*check if it gets enough…, see if it needs / wants more / less…, make sure that the room isn't…*)

____

3 Your friend has an apple tree that has delicious apples. You want a tree just like it.

(*take seeds from…, ask what kind of tree…*)

____

Unit 3

Living Things

THE BIG ? How do living things grow and change?

1 What are the names of these adult and young animals? Label the photos.

1 f _r_ o _g_

a c __ t __ __ __ i __ __ a __

2 __ __ t __ __ __ __ f __ y

b j __ e __ __

3 k __ __ g __ __ __ o

c __ a __ __ o __ e

2 Who belongs to whom? Match the adult animals 1–3 above, with their young a–c.

3 Can you answer these questions? Think about the animals in the photos.

1 Which animal can live in the water and on land? _______________

2 Which animal carries its young in a pouch on the front of its body? _______________

3 Which animal's young look very different from its parents? _______________

Make sure you understand the main idea of a text. To help you do that, underline the most important words in the text.

4 What do young humans need to grow? What do young animals need? Are they the same?

____

____

5 Which title? Read the text quickly, and write the title in the space below.

a How Baby Animals Grow   **b** Animal Families

____

Human babies have families to look after them. They need lots of help when they are small. They cannot do anything alone! Animals are different. Some animals can look after themselves from the first day of their lives. Many animals only stay with their mothers for a short time, and many animals never even see their fathers. But there are some animal fathers that stay and look after their young. Here is one of them. A seahorse father keeps his babies in a pouch on the front of his body, like kangaroo mothers do. The young seahorses stay there for about two months.

6 The young and their parents. Read the text again and circle the correct word.

1 Human babies can do **more** / **fewer** things than most animal babies.

2 Animal fathers **don't usually** / **never** stay with their young.

3 Seahorse babies live inside their father's **pouch** / **body**.

7 Which animal and its young do you know most about? Write sentences.

What we call the young animals.   A ____________ has ____________.

What the baby animals can/cannot do.   They can ____________.
They cannot ____________.

How the parent looks after the young.   Mother/Father ____________ and
____________ the ____________.

Lesson 1 · What are the life cycles of some animals?

1 How long do you think butterflies live? Choose a, b, or c. Read the text to find out.

a One to two years.　　**b** Two to eight months.　　**c** Two to four weeks.

2 What can you remember about a butterfly's life cycle? Read the text and complete the diagram.

A butterfly has a short life cycle. From beginning to end, a butterfly's life lasts between two and eight months. Usually, bigger butterflies live longer than smaller butterflies.

The butterfly begins its life as an egg. The larva, or caterpillar, develops inside the egg. After seven to ten days, the egg hatches. The next stage is called the larva stage, and it lasts two to four weeks. The larva eats a lot to store energy. Next, a hard covering, called a chrysalis, forms around the larva. This stage is called the pupa stage. The chrysalis protects it while the pupa develops into a butterfly. This stage takes ten to fifteen days. Finally, the adult butterfly comes out of the chrysalis. An adult female finds a mate. Then it can lay eggs. It usually lays its eggs on the plants the caterpillar is going to eat. An adult butterfly can live for about three to four weeks.

1 Stage: _____egg_____
What happens:
The larva develops inside the egg.

2 Stage: __________
What happens:

3 Stage: __________
What happens:

4 Stage: __________
What happens:

3 What can you remember about a frog's life cycle? Put the stages a–d in the correct order.

☐ **a** The tadpole grows legs, and its tail becomes shorter. The tadpole develops lungs, and its gills disappear. This stage takes 12–16 weeks.

☐ **b** After 6–21 days, the tadpole hatches. The tadpole breathes with gills, like fish do.

☐ **c** The adult frog is an amphibian. It lives on land and in water. It finds a mate and lays eggs in the water. It reproduces many times before it dies.

☐ **d** The female frog lays hundreds or thousands of eggs in the water.

4 What makes a butterfly and a frog different? Complete the chart.

Butterfly	Frog
1 It's _an insect_ (type of animal).	**1** It's ___________ (type of animal).
2 To reproduce, it ___________ ___________ on ___________.	**2** To reproduce, it ___________ ___________ in ___________.
3 The eggs take ___________ to hatch.	**3** The eggs take ___________ to hatch.
4 There are four stages: egg, ___________, ___________, adult.	**4** There are four stages: ___________, ___________, growing tadpole, ___________.

5 The life cycle of a tadpole. Match to put the stages in the correct order.

1 First,	a	the tadpole breathes with lungs.
2 Next,	b	the tadpole breathes with gills.
3 Finally,	c	thick skin begins to cover the gills and lungs develop.

6 Which comes first? Write sentences in the correct order of the stages. Use *First*, *Next*, and *Finally*.

1 Life Cycle of a Mammal

baby / is born

egg / develop / inside the mother's body

baby / grow / into an adult

First, the egg develops inside the mother's body. Next,...

____

2 Young Animal and Growth

kitten / grow into / adult and can feed itself

kitten / drink only milk from its mother

kitten / can eat / the food its mother brings

____

____

3 Adult Animal and Reproduction

kitten / become / an adult bobcat

it / reproduce

it / find / a mate

____

____

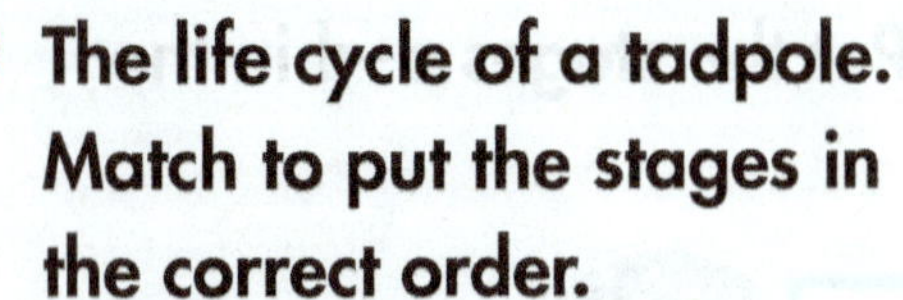

Lesson 2 · How can you classify animals?

1 **There are many different characteristics we use to classify animals. Match the characteristics 1–6 with the examples a–f.**

1 physical characteristic   **a** the animal has a backbone

2 behavior   **b** the animal's body temperature stays the same even when its environment is hot or cold

3 vertebrate   **c** the animal has a specific body feature like scales, a hard shell, or fur

4 invertebrate   **d** the animal does not have a backbone

5 cold-blooded   **e** the animal behaves in a specific way: it eats only plants, or it sleeps during the day

6 warm-blooded   **f** the animal's body temperature depends on the temperature of its environment

2 **Different ways to group animals. Label, using words from the box.**

> warm-blooded   lay eggs   arthropods   cold-blooded
> have scales   ~~vertebrates~~   have live births   invertebrates

1 [vertebrates]
fish amphibians reptiles birds mammals

2 [ ]
sea jellies worms mollusks arthropods

3 [ ]
most fish amphibians reptiles

4 [ ]
birds mammals

5 [ ]
fish reptiles

6 [ ]
fish amphibians reptiles birds

7 [ ]
mammals a few reptiles

8 [ ]
spiders crabs insects

3 Describing animals. Look at the photos and answer the questions.

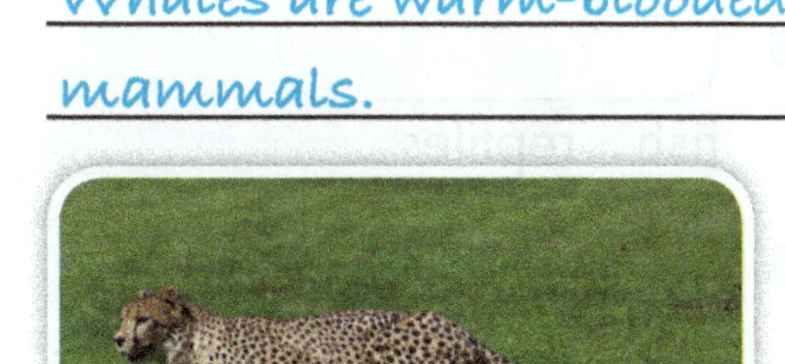

Which of these animals…

1 is an arthropod? ____________

2 are invertebrates? ____________

3 is a cold-blooded vertebrate? ____________

> **Grammar Tip**
>
> Snakes **are cold-blooded** vertebrates.
> Elephants **are large** mammals.

4 Describing animals. Make the two sentences into one sentence.

1 Whales are warm-blooded. Whales are mammals.

<u>Whales are warm-blooded mammals.</u>

2 Dolphins are playful. Dolphins are animals.

____

____

3 Cheetahs are runners. They are fast.

____

____

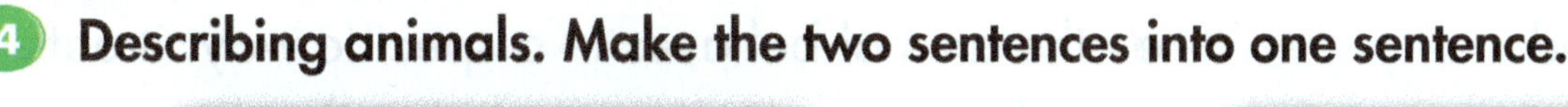

4 Clams are mollusks. They are hard-shelled.

____

____

5 Which of the traits in **4** are physical? Which traits have to do with behavior? Write the numbers below.

Physical: _______________________   Behavior: _______________________

6 How can we describe these animals? Complete the sentences using a form of *be* + *a/an* + adjective. Use adjectives from the box.

warm-blooded
soft-bodied
egg-laying
hard-shelled
tall
intelligent

sea jelly

orangutan

1 A giraffe _____*is a tall*_____ animal.

2 A crab _____________ arthropod.

3 A mammal _____________ vertebrate.

4 A sea jelly _____________ invertebrate.

5 A crocodile _____________ reptile.

6 An orangutan _____________ mammal.

7 How about you? Write a fun paragraph about you for the school website.

The 'Animals' of Class _____________

Hi, my name's _________________.

The group of animals I belong to is _____________________.

Physical Traits:

I (don't) look like _______________________.

I am _______________________.

I have _______________________.

Behavior Traits:

I can/can't _______________________.

I'm good/bad at _______________________.

Review 1–3

1 What can you remember? Do the quiz. Circle a, b, or c.

1 We use a lever to ___.
- **a** cut through material
- **b** lift and move things
- **c** connect a lower level to a higher level

2 A can opener is ___.

- **a** not a machine
- **b** a simple machine
- **c** a complex machine

3 The design process is a step-by-step method used to ___.
- **a** find a solution to a problem
- **b** do research
- **c** test new products

4 Pollination happens when ___.
- **a** pollen moves to the part of the plant that makes seeds
- **b** the wind blows pollen away from the pine cones
- **c** fruit grows around the seeds

5 Which part of the plant does NOT grow in the ground?
- **a** the stem
- **b** the flower
- **c** the seed

6 Invertebrates do not ___.
- **a** live on land
- **b** produce eggs
- **c** have a backbone

7 Amphibians ___.
- **a** have lungs when they are adults
- **b** have lungs when they are young
- **c** have gills when they are adults

8 A snake is a ___.
- **a** cold-blooded vertebrate
- **b** warm-blooded vertebrate
- **c** cold-blooded invertebrate

You get one point for each correct answer. What's your score?

1–2 Not good   **3–6** OK   **7–8** Excellent

2 **What is it? Write the words.**

1 The body of a fish is covered with them. (noun) _____________

2 A feature, e.g. eye color, that parents pass on to their child. (noun)_____________

3 What plants and animals do when they make new plants or have young animals. (verb) _____________

4 Seeds do this to produce a new plant. (verb) _____________

5 What a butterfly goes through as it changes from a caterpillar to a pupa to a butterfly. (noun) _____________

6 This simple machine is an inclined plane wrapped around a center post. It is used to hold things together. (noun) _____________

7 The way living things behave. (noun) _____________

8 Plants need them to live and grow. They come from the soil. Minerals belong to this group. (noun) _____________

3 **Which is the odd one out? Circle and explain why it does not belong to the group.**

1 results   research   hatch   prototype   engineer
All the other words are related to _______________________________.

2 chrysalis   pupa   amphibian   larva   insect
All the other words are related to _______________________________.

3 stem   root   mollusk   petal   cactus
All the other words are related to _______________________________.

4 octopus   sea jelly   squid   spider   fish
All the other animals are _______________________________.

5 to construct   to evaluate   to research   to germinate   to design
All the other words are related to _______________________________.

Unit 4 Ecosystems

How do living things interact?

1 **What are these words relating to ecosystems? Unscramble the letters.**

arni otsref

rain forest

ihtgulns

____

slsrgadna

____

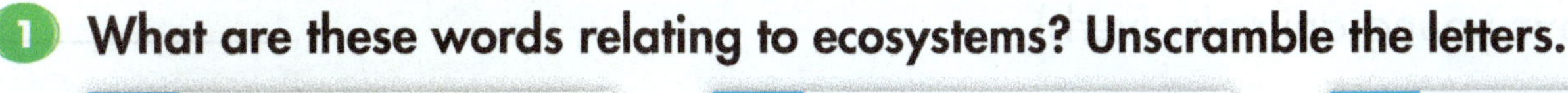

ocarl erfe

____

lios

____

hrasm

____

2 **Where do living things get food and energy from? Match.**

plants   animals

sunlight   other animals   soil   plants

3 **What can you remember about ecosystems? Complete the text with words from 1. You must use the plural for some words.**

Ecosystems

(1) _Grasslands_ get their name because they are covered in grasses and other short plants. They are called prairies in North America, steppes in Asia, and savannahs in Africa. It doesn't rain much in these places, so the **(2)** ___________ is very dry. Not many trees grow because there isn't enough water.

(3) ___________ are found in oceans all over the world. They are very important because many different sea animals live there. Corals look like plants, but they are actually collections of tiny simple animals.

(4) ___________ are forest ecosystems where it rains a lot. They have very tall trees, and are home to about 30 million different plants and animals. The trees don't let in much **(5)** ___________, so it is usually dark at the bottom of the forest.

4 **Which animals live in each of the ecosystems in 3? Fill in the gaps.**

1 giraffe
2 clam
3 sea star
4 frog
5 lion
6 beetle

1 The ___________ and the ___________ live in ___________ ecosystem.

2 The ___________ and the ___________ live in ___________ ecosystem.

3 The ___________ and the ___________ live in ___________ ecosystem.

5 **An interesting ecosystem. Write.**

I find the ___________ the most interesting because ___________
___________.

What would you like to see/do there?
I would like to ___________
___________.

Lesson 1 · What is an ecosystem?

1 **Which word is correct? Read the definitions. Circle the right answer.**

1 When living and nonliving parts of an environment interact, this is called a(n) **wetland** / **ecosystem**.

2 The place where a living thing makes its home is its **habitat** / **population**.

3 All the living things of the same kind that live in the same place make up a **group** / **population**.

4 All the different populations that live in the same place make up a **community** / **family**.

5 A living or nonliving thing does something. This makes a difference to another living or nonliving thing. The verb we use to describe this is **attract** / **interact**.

6 When one thing needs another thing to help it live and grow, we say that it **depends on** / **shelters** it.

2 **Ecosystems. Read the notes and complete with words in bold from 1. You must use the plural of some nouns and change the form of a verb.**

- Different living things make their homes in different (**1**) _habitats_.
- The type of the land and the climate create different (**2**) _______________. The living and nonliving things that we find in a desert are different from those that we find in a rain forest.
- We find large (**3**) _______________ of the same living things in one place because the conditions are right for them.
- Living things cannot survive alone. They (**4**) _______________ on nonliving things and also on other living things in their (**5**) _______________.
- Because they share the same environment, living and nonliving things (**6**) _______________ with one another. For example, big trees give birds shelter. The fish in a river are food for meat-eating animals.

3 **Which adjective fits? Make adjectives from the words in the box to complete the text.**

eat   amaze   interact   live   interest   excite   surprise

The (1) _Amazing_ Life of Rain Forests

Tropical rain forests have a large number of different populations of (**2**) _____________ things. We find about 50% of all the plants and animals on Earth in rain forests. People often make (**3**) _____________ discoveries in rain forests, like finding completely new insects and plants that nobody knew about before. That's why rain forests are really (**4**) _____________ places for scientists!

Here's an (**5**) _____________ fact about rain forests. Plants and animals live in (**6**) _____________ communities, and they often help one another. For example, some plants give shelter to ants. The ants protect them from leaf-(**7**) _____________ insects, and the ants have a home, so everyone's happy!

4 **The African savannah. Write sentences. Don't forget to make adjectives, correct verb forms, and add small words like *a*, *the*, and *of*.**

1 The African savannah / be / tropical grassland
The African savannah is a tropical grassland.

2 Around two million / plant-eat / mammals / live in / savannah
____

3 There be / different types / plant-eat animals / because / there be / different types / plants
____

4 Some animals, / like zebras, / eat / grass. / Others, / like giraffes, / eat / leaves.
____

Lesson 2 · How do living things get energy?

1 Links in the food chain. Think and write yes or no.

Do you think that some links are more important than others? ____________

2 What can you remember? Read the text again and find the names of three decomposers.

____

Food Chain Q&A

Q: Decomposers are horrible! They get energy from waste, dead plants, and dead animals. Yuck! Do we really need them? (Kayla, 9)

A: Imagine an ecosystem without decomposers. It's a place full of dead plants and animals. There's no place for new life to grow. There's animal waste everywhere. (Now, that's yucky!) Mushrooms, bacteria (really small forms of life), and earthworms clean all this up. Do you still think we can do without them?

Q: Are decomposers part of the food chain? (Vas, 10)

A: Yes, they are. Every link in the food chain is important. When decomposers, like earthworms, break down dead matter or waste, it turns into nutrients and minerals in the soil. Producers use sunlight and water to make sugar, but they cannot grow without these nutrients. Without decomposers, producers cannot stay alive. The food chain breaks because, without producers, there's no food for consumers. This means that the ecosystem is destroyed.

3 True or false? Circle _T_ (true) or _F_ (false).

1 Decomposers make room for new plants to grow.　　　　T / F

2 Producers are the most important link in the food chain.　　　　T / F

3 Producers can make all their own nutrients.　　　　T / F

4 The ecosystem is destroyed when the food chain breaks.　　　　T / F

4 Which kinds of consumer are they? Write the names of the animals in the correct part of the diagram.

1 A **lion** eats zebras and lizards.

2 A **dog** eats rice and beef.

3 A **prairie dog** eats grass.

4 A **gorilla** eats leaves and fruit.

5 A **turtle** eats worms and plants.

6 A **cat** eats mice and birds.

Herbivores   Omnivores   Carnivores

Lion

__________   __________   __________

__________   __________   __________

5 Can you join them together? Use the information below. Use different colors for different food chains. Draw lines to make food chains.

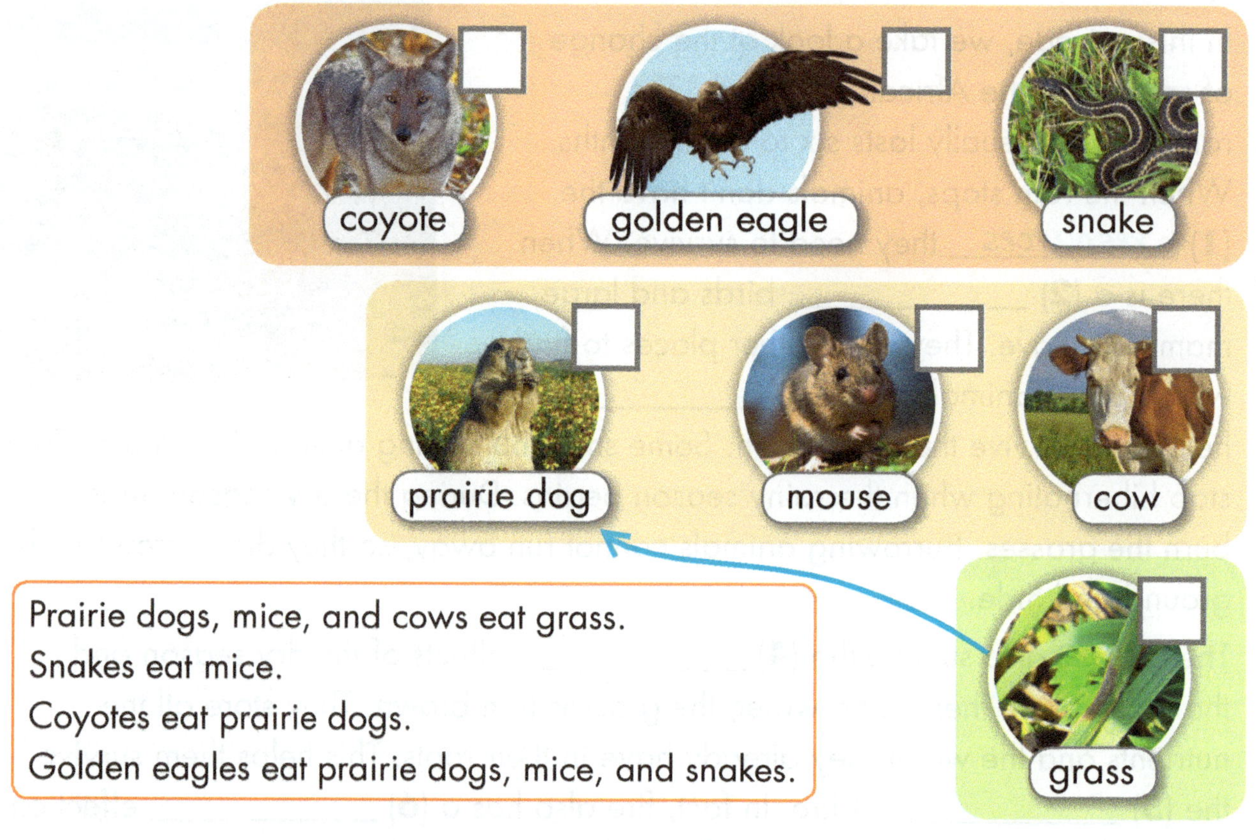

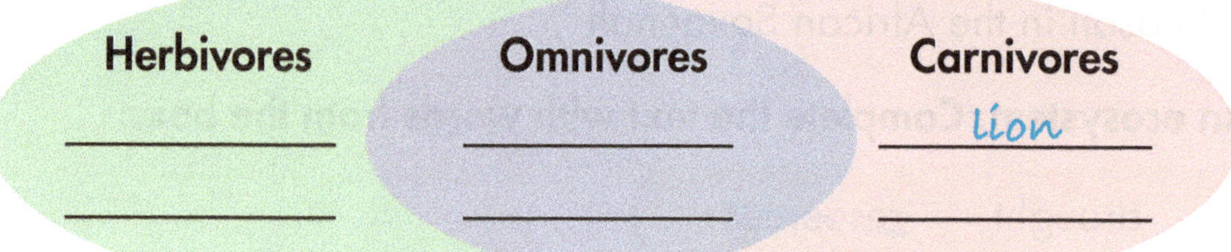

Prairie dogs, mice, and cows eat grass.
Snakes eat mice.
Coyotes eat prairie dogs.
Golden eagles eat prairie dogs, mice, and snakes.

6 Producer (P) or consumer (C)? Label the photos in **5**.

Lesson 3 · How do ecosystems change?

1 **What is the best title for episode 4? Read the summary and write the title in the space below.**

a Plants and Animals of the Savannah

b Plant and Animal Adaptation in the Savannah

c The Rainy Season in the African Savannah

2 **Changes in an ecosystem. Complete the text with words from the box.**

negative   drought   resources
adaptations   effects   positive

The Secret Life of Ecosystems   Tuesday, 17:30

Episode 4: ______________________________

In this episode, we take a look at the change of seasons in the African savannah. The rainy season usually lasts six to eight months. When the rain stops, animals don't have the **(1)** _resources_ they need to survive. When there is a **(2)** ____________, birds and large mammals move. They go to other places to find water. Some animals have **(3)** ____________ that help them survive the dry season. Some small burrowing animals hibernate. They stop hibernating when the rainy season begins. During the dry season, fires often burn the grasses. Burrowing animals cannot run away, so they dig burrows in the ground and hide.

The grasses also survive the **(4)** ____________ effects of the dry season and the fires. When there is no water, the grasses turn brown. They store all the nutrients and the water they already have in their roots. This helps them survive the **(5)** ____________ of fire. In fact, fire also has a **(6)** ____________ effect on grasses because the ash from the fire makes the soil rich in nutrients.

3 **Which word—*always*, *never*, *usually*, or *often*? Use the symbols as a guide.**

1 Animals ___usually___ look for different foods to eat, to get different nutrients. ✓✓✓

2 Birds ___________ make their nests on trees. ✓✓

3 The grasses ___________ stay green during the dry season. ✗

4 It ___________ rains every day during the rainy season. ✓✓✓

5 Fallen trees ___________ provide a habitat for living organisms. ✓✓✓✓

6 The soil ___________ becomes richer in nutrients after a flood. ✓✓

Grammar Tip

Ecosystems are **always** changing. ✓✓✓✓
Fallen trees **usually** provide a habitat for small animals. ✓✓✓
Other animals **often** live in burrows made by groundhogs. ✓✓
It **never** rains during a drought. ✗

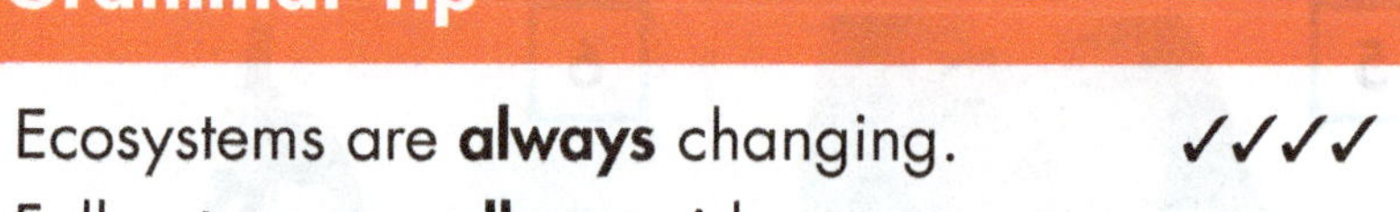

4 **Marshes. Write sentences. Use the text in 2 as a guide.**

1 marshes / found at the edges / lakes and rivers. (often)
Marshes are often found at the edges of lakes and rivers.

2 covered with water. (always) / water / rich in nutrients. (always)

3 living organisms / have adaptations / help them survive / flooded conditions. / for example, / plants / tall, / like grasses and reeds. (usually)

Unit 5 — Body and Illness

How can I keep my body healthy?

1 What can you see in the photos? Write the missing letters.

1 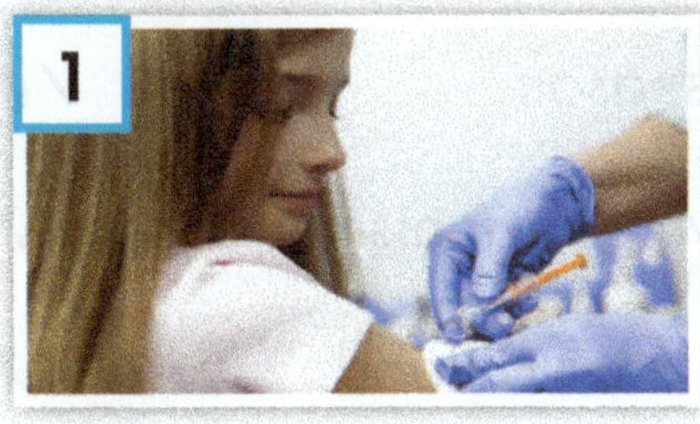 v a c c i n e

2 _ _ _ qu _ t _

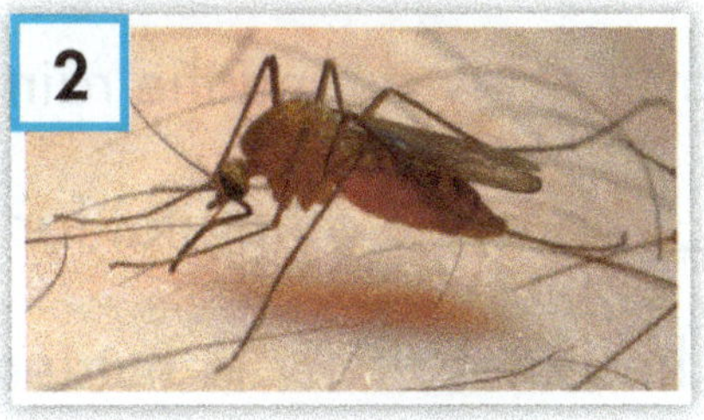

3  s _ _ e _ e

4 _ a _ t _ _ _ a

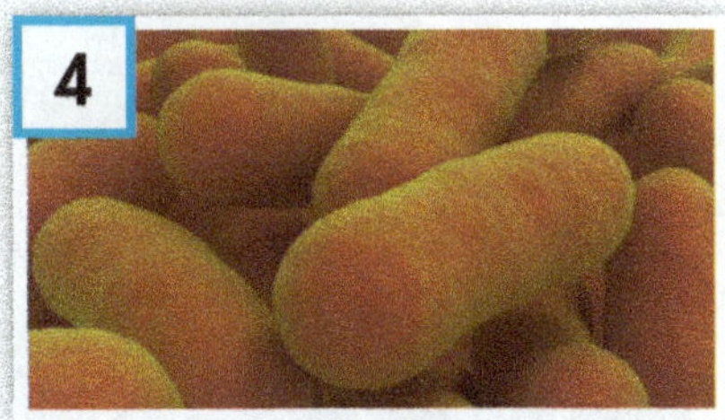

5 _ _ v _ r

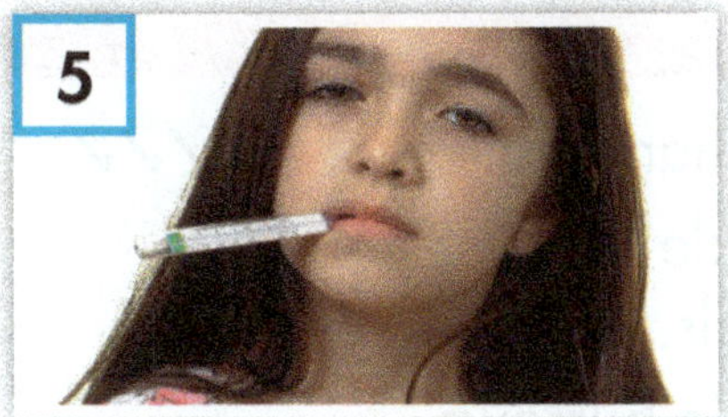

6 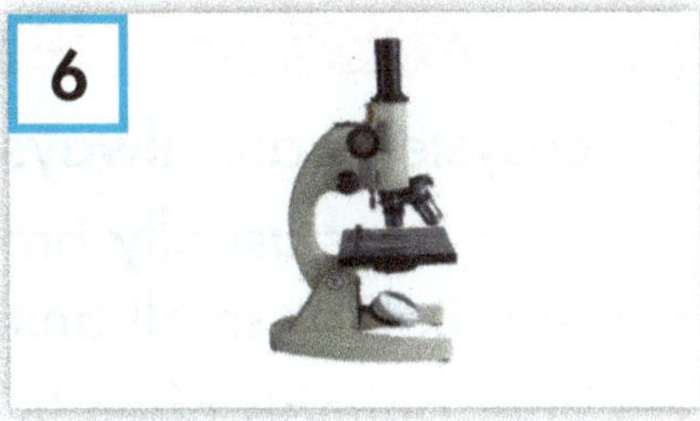 m _ c _ _ _ _ c _ p _

2 What do these words mean? Match the words (1–6) from **1** to the definitions (a–f).

a [3] When air comes out of your nose with great force. (*verb*)

b [ ] When you have a very high temperature. (*noun*)

c [ ] An insect that can pass diseases to humans. (*noun*)

d [ ] It can help stop a disease from passing from one person to another. (*noun*)

e [ ] An instrument that makes things look much larger. (*noun*)

f [ ] Very small organisms that we cannot see. Some of them can make us sick. (*noun*)

3 Where does the text in **4** come from? Look at the layout and photos and mark (✓) the correct answer.

a a website for adults ☐

b a book for doctors to tell kids what to do ☐

c an information poster for kids ☐

4 Healthy habits. Match the points (1–6) with the photos (a–f).

1 Get enough sleep. When you are tired you get sick more easily. ☐ b

2 Eat well. Your body needs the right nutrients to stay healthy. It's easy to get them from different types of food like vegetables, meat, milk, and grains. ☐

3 Drink water. Five to eight glasses a day is usually enough. When you have a fever, drink more. It will help you feel better, too. ☐

4 Wash your hands before you eat. This will kill bacteria. ☐

5 Stay away from people who sneeze and cover your nose and mouth when you sneeze. If you are sick, stay in bed and rest! ☐

6 Get your vaccines. Vaccines protect us from lots of dangerous diseases. They don't just stop you from getting sick, they can save your life. ☐

5 What about you? Which of the things in **4** do you or don't you do?

I ____.

I don't ____.

Lesson 1 · What causes different diseases?

1 Getting sick. Complete the chart with words from the box.

> bacteria   allergies   flower pollen   viruses
> toxins   the flu   a broken arm   sneezing

Infectious Diseases	Noninfectious Diseases	Injuries
strep throat	(2) ___________	(3) ___________
(1) ___the flu___	asthma	a cut finger
chickenpox	diabetes	sunburn
Caused by pathogens	**Caused by allergens**	
(4) ___________	(6) ___________	
(5) ___________	air pollution	
parasites	dust	
fungi	tobacco smoke	
Effect	**Effect**	
attack cells	body works in an abnormal way	
make (7) ___________ to	(8) ___________ and coughing	
attack cells	rash	
infection	difficult to breathe	

2 What do you know about chickenpox? Have you had it? When?

Chickenpox is ____.

I ____.

3 Where does it come from? Read the text in 4 and mark (✓) the correct answer.

a a kids' magazine ☐

b a website with advice about health ☐

c a website for doctors ☐

4 Talking about chickenpox. Choose words from the box to complete the text. You don't need all the words.

fever　　virus　　allergen　　noninfectious disease　　infectious disease
toxin　　vaccination　　immune system　　microorganism

Chickenpox	Symptoms	Causes	What to Do	When to See a Doctor

Chickenpox is a common (**1**) _________________. It is caused by a (**2**) _________________, called varicella-zoster.

Most children catch it at some stage in their lives. Chickenpox causes a rash with red spots. Some children have only a few spots. Other children have a lot of spots, all over their bodies.

Some children have a (**3**) _________________ for the first two days. Because chickenpox is so common, most adults are immune to it because they have had it as children. The (**4**) _________________ of children is better at fighting the disease. When adults get chickenpox, it can be more serious.

That's why adults who didn't have the disease as children should get a chickenpox (**5**) _________________.

5 What do you think is wrong with these children? Read the texts and answer the questions.

I went downtown yesterday. There were lots of cars in the streets.
I felt like I couldn't breathe, and I had to use my inhaler.　(Cedric, 10)

1 What do you think is wrong with Cedric? _________________
Is it an infectious disease? _________________
Will the same thing happen again? Why? _________________

My uncle just came back from a trip to Africa. He said there were a lot of mosquitoes there and they bit him. He is not feeling well now. He has a fever and is very tired all the time.　(Denise, 10)

2 What do you think Denise's uncle has? _________________
How did he get it? _________________

6 Talking about different things. Read the text in 4 again. Find the sentences with *some, other,* and *most,* and underline them.

7 Infectious diseases. Complete the text with *some, other, most.* Then answer the question at the end of the text: *I think…*

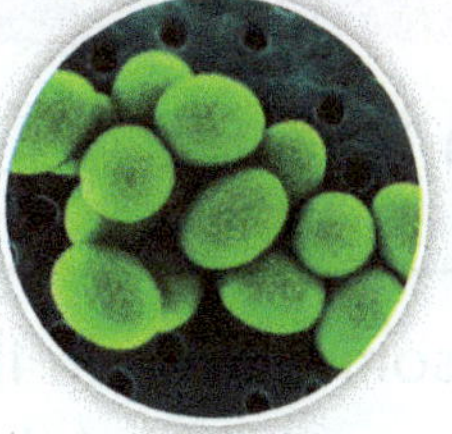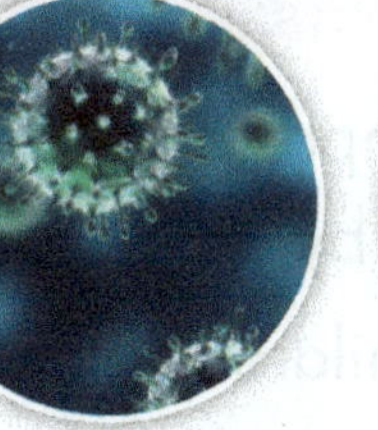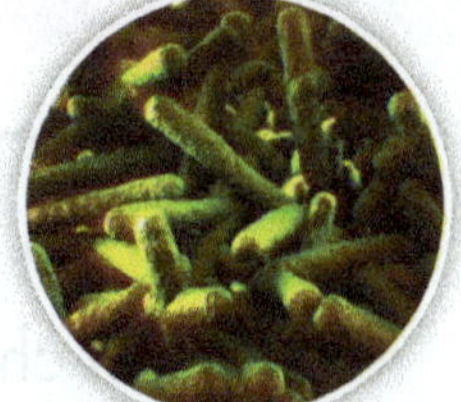

(1) _____Most_____ infectious diseases are passed on from one person to another. (2) _____________ people are very careful, but they can become sick.
(3) _____________ people are not very careful, but they don't often get sick. These people have very strong immune systems.
(4) _____________ people catch a cold at some time in their life. (5) _____________ people don't change what they do. They still go to work or go to school.
(6) _____________ people stay at home and rest. Who do you think gets well sooner? Why?
I think ____.

8 The flu. Write, using the information below. Follow the text in 4 as a model.

Type of disease: infectious, common	**Cause:** different viruses
Who gets it: most people	
Vaccine: yes (especially for old people and young children)	
How you feel: fever, sneeze, cough, feeling tired, body hurts some people feel very sick, other people fight the disease better	

The flu is ____
____
____

Lesson 2 · How can you avoid getting diseases?

1 How diseases spread. Draw lines to match 1–6 with a–f.

1 In the past, people didn't know what caused a disease or how it spread.

2 Some infectious diseases are caused by bacteria that are found in uncooked meat, like chicken.

3 Another way diseases can spread is from one person to another.

4 Other diseases are spread when an infected animal or insect bites a person.

5 Diseases are also spread when people touch contaminated objects.

6 There are many serious diseases that are carried in water.

a Cold and flu viruses spread in the air when infected people sneeze.

b Fungal infections, like athlete's foot, can spread this way.

c As a result, they didn't know how to avoid it.

d Cholera is a dangerous disease that spreads when people drink dirty water.

e Rabies and malaria are two examples.

f This is why many people died of food poisoning caused by *Salmonella*.

2 Which diseases are linked to what is shown in the photos? Write.

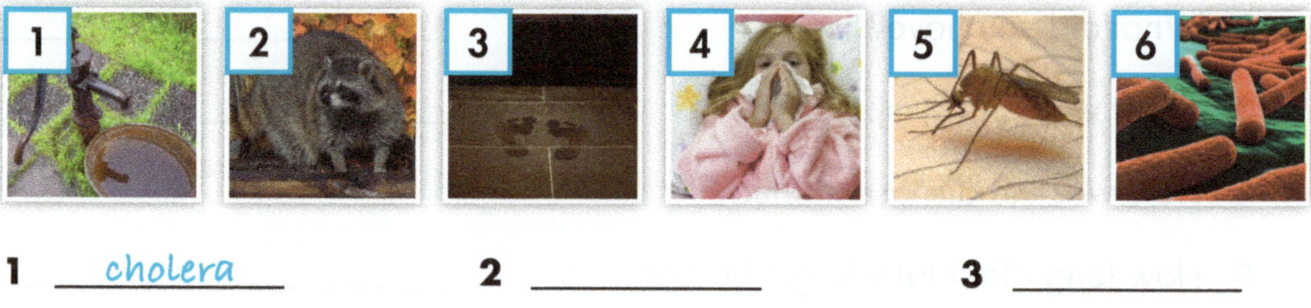

1 cholera

2 __________

3 __________

4 __________

5 __________

6 __________

3 **Treating and preventing diseases. Circle the correct words.**

Medicines like (**1**) **antibiotics** / **antibodies** can kill most bacterial infections. There are many different types of (**2**) **viruses** / **antibiotics** because there are many different types of bacteria. You can recover from some diseases like (**3**) *Salmonella* / **asthma** without antibiotics. Doctors treat the (**4**) **chronic disease** / **symptoms of the disease**, like throwing up or diarrhea. This way, they help the (**5**) **infected** / **healthy** person's immune system fight the bacteria.

Viral infections are not (**6**) **treated** / **infected** with antibiotics. The only way to avoid a disease caused by a virus is to have a(n) (**7**) **infection** / **vaccination** before you get infected. When the vaccine is injected into your bloodstream, your immune system creates (**8**) **antibodies** / **vaccines** to fight and kill the virus. Your body remembers how to create these antibodies. If the virus attacks you in the future, the antibodies will protect you. There are different types of vaccines for different types of viruses.

(**9**) **Chronic** / **Noninfectious** diseases don't go away. Doctors can give medicine to treat the (**10**) **health** / **symptoms**. People with these kinds of diseases make changes in their lives to stop the disease from causing other problems or from getting worse.

4 **What about you? Answer these questions.**

1 When was the last time you were sick? ______________________

2 What did you have? ______________________

3 What were the symptoms? ______________________

4 How was the disease treated? ______________________

5 How long did it take to get better? ______________________

6 What can you do to avoid getting sick again?

____

5 Disease and infection. Write sentences using *can/cannot*.

> **Grammar Tip**
>
> Washing your hands **can** help you stay healthy. A person **cannot** pass a noninfectious disease to another person.

1 viruses, bacteria, and fungi / live / on our hands

Viruses, bacteria, and fungi can live on our hands.

2 you / get infected / by touching your nose, eyes, and mouth

3 you / take / antibiotics without asking your doctor first

4 you / get / a fungal infection if you touch a contaminated object

5 you / be / with other people if you have a highly infectious disease

6 Can these things happen? Write sentences, using *can* or *cannot*.

1 Can pathogens live in the soil?

Yes, pathogens can live in the soil.

2 Can some pathogens spread without touching the infected person?

3 Can you treat a disease caused by a virus with antibiotics?

4 Can you treat a fungal infection with antifungal cream?

5 Can you have an infectious disease without having symptoms?

Unit 6 — Earth and Weather

How do forces cause changes on Earth's surface?

1 Can you remember these words about Earth and weather?
Unscramble the words in the box and label the photos.

aehtaequkr   wson   ahter   ludcso   ~~ahli~~   adlsnidle

hail

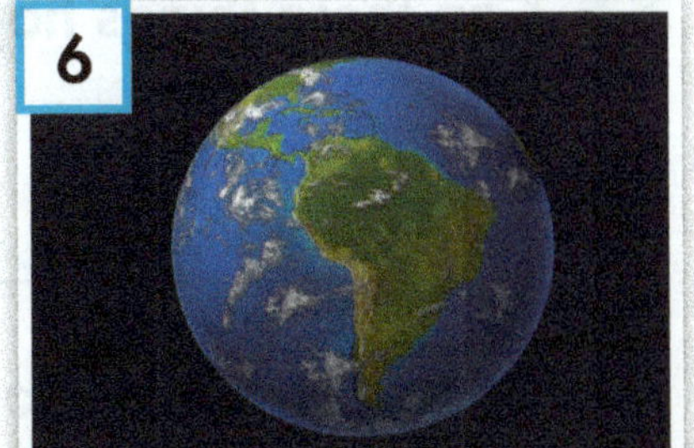

2 How do the things shown in the photos cause changes on Earth's surface?
Complete with words from 1.

(1) _____________ produce rain, snow, and hail that fall on Earth's surface.

(2) _____________ and (3) _____________ melt
and fill up Earth's water reserves:
groundwater, lakes, rivers, and oceans.

(4) _____________ and (5) _____________
change how Earth's surface looks.

3 Our changing planet. Read the text and complete with one word in each space. The first letter of each word is given.

(1) E_arth's_ surface has changed many times since the beginning of time. New islands came out of the sea, and dry land was covered with water. Some mountains slowly disappeared, and new ones appeared somewhere else.

Earth's surface is still changing. Sometimes the (2) c___________ are fast. Some changes come from the inside, like when an (3) e___________ shakes the ground and makes islands appear out of nowhere. Others happen from the outside, like when a (4) l___________ brings down the side of a mountain. Most changes are slow, and they happen over a very long time. We can only see the changes if we look at old maps, photos, or paintings of the same area from different (5) t___________ in the past. Slow changes are caused by moving water and wind. (6) W___________ never stops moving. It rises from Earth's surface to the air, where it becomes a (7) c___________. It comes back to Earth as rain, snow, or (8) h___________, and fills up the rivers that run into the oceans. Wind moves pieces of rock and soil from one place to another.

There is nothing we can do about natural changes. What we can do is try to stay safe from sudden changes and learn how to live with slow ones.

4 How can these changes to Earth's surface affect people's lives? Write three sentences. Use as many of these phrases as you want.

destroys crops/towns/villages   causes buildings to collapse
makes road conditions dangerous   pollutes water/air
damages cars/buildings   injures/kills people and animals

1 An earthquake ____

____.

2 A landslide ____

____.

3 Hail ____

____.

Lesson 1 · What is the water cycle?

1 **The water cycle. What do the pictures show? Label the stages shown in the photos.**

precipitation   condensation   storage   evaporation

The Water Cycle

______________   ______________   ______________   ______________

2 **Describing the water cycle. Circle the correct words.**

a The heat from the sun causes water to become rain / water vapor and rise into the air. _evaporation_

b Water vapor cools down / heats up and it becomes liquid again. Tiny water droplets form clouds. ______________

c Water particles / Clouds join together. They become heavy and fall to Earth as rain, snow, sleet, or hail. ______________

d Some water seeps into the ground. Some water flows over the land, and evaporates / collects in streams, lakes, and oceans. ______________

3 **Which stage in the water cycle? Write the stages to match the descriptions, in 2 above.**

4 **What happens? Read the descriptions. Choose *condensation* or *evaporation*.**

1 You put wet clothes near a heater.   condensation / evaporation

2 You have a very hot shower and the bathroom mirror is covered with tiny droplets of water.   condensation / evaporation

3 You put a glass in the freezer. When you take it out ten minutes later, the glass looks cloudy.   condensation / evaporation

5 **Where are the texts from? Read and choose a source from the box. There are two extra sources.**

personal email   school essay
poster advert   newspaper article

1 ___________

Temperatures steady in the low 60s. South winds at 10 to 20 mph. Chance of precipitation 50%, mostly in the late afternoon.

2 ___________

Don't worry, there's nothing wrong with your windows.

I had the same problem recently. This happens when the vapor in the warm air from inside the room touches the cold glass of the window and changes to water. What you can do is leave one of the windows a little bit open. You can also turn up the heat in the room, so the air in the room moves more and the water dries more quickly.

Hope that helps!

6 **Which one is correct? Read the texts in 5 again. Circle the right answer, a, b, or c.**

1 Text 1: Is it going to rain in the afternoon?

  a No, it's not.   **b** Yes, it is.   **c** It may rain.

2 Text 2: What is the problem with the windows?

  a Condensation forms.   **b** There is precipitation.
  c They let water evaporate.

3 Text 2: What is the solution?

  a Leave all the windows open.
  b Make the air cooler inside.
  c Make the air warmer inside and open one of the windows.

Lesson 2 • How do we describe features of Earth's surface?

1 **Earthquakes and volcanoes. What's missing? Read the text and complete with words from the box.**

> cracks   crater   crust   erupt   lava
> melted rock   mountains   waves

The outer surface of Earth is a layer of rock called the
(1) _____crust_____. But this rock does not cover its
surface in one piece. Imagine big dinner plates that float on
(2) _____________. Earthquakes happen when the dinner
plates shift or move and hit one another. Big earthquakes
can open large **(3)** _____________ (called faults) in the crust, and cause
landslides. They can also cause huge ocean **(4)** _____________ that can do a lot
of damage when they hit the land.

Both volcanoes and earthquakes cause sudden and rapid changes. Volcanoes
are part of Earth's crust. They are landforms that look like **(5)** _____________,
but with a hole called a **(6)** _____________ at the top. When volcanoes
(7) _____________, melted rock pushes up through the crater with force, like
frosting pushed out of a bag. The melted rock comes from the layer below Earth's
crust, and is called **(8)** _____________. As it flows down the volcano's side, it
creates a landslide. A very hot one!

2 **Are these facts true for volcanoes or for earthquakes, or for both?**
Read the text in 1 again and complete the table.

		volcanoes	earthquakes
1	They begin below Earth's crust.	✓	X
2	They can change the shape of Earth's surface.		
3	They cause rapid changes.		
4	They are landforms.		
5	They can make faults appear in Earth's surface.		

3 **Which is correct? Circle the right word.**

1 The San Andreas Fault is **in** / **on** California.

2 There's often snow **on** / **next to** high mountain tops.

3 The sky is always blue **in** / **above** the rain clouds.

4 The climate **next to** / **on** the ocean is usually very pleasant.

5 Glaciers form **in** / **above** cold places like the Arctic.

4 **What's missing? Complete with *in, on, above,* or *next to.***

1 Bodies of water are one type of feature found ____________ Earth's surface.

2 A mountain is a landform high ____________ the land around it.

3 About 97% of the water on our planet is ____________ the oceans.

4 The soil ____________ a volcano is rich in nutrients.

5 **Rapid changes to Earth's surface. Write sentences.**

1 volcano / be / opening / in / Earth's crust.

____

2 hot, melted rock / come out of / volcano / when / it / erupt.

____

3 most earthquakes / happen / along / faults.

____

4 ground / shake / during / earthquake.

____

Lesson 3 · What are weathering and erosion?

1 **Which is correct? Circle the right word.**

1 **weathering** / **erosion**: The process that moves weathered material away from where it came originally.

2 **weathering** / **erosion**: Any process that breaks material like rock into small pieces.

2 **What do these photos show? Match words (1–7) with photos (a–g).**

1 glacier   [f]

2 erosion by gravity   [ ]

3 erosion by wind   [ ]

4 erosion by water   [ ]

5 weathering by plants   [ ]

6 weathering by water   [ ]

7 deposition   [ ]

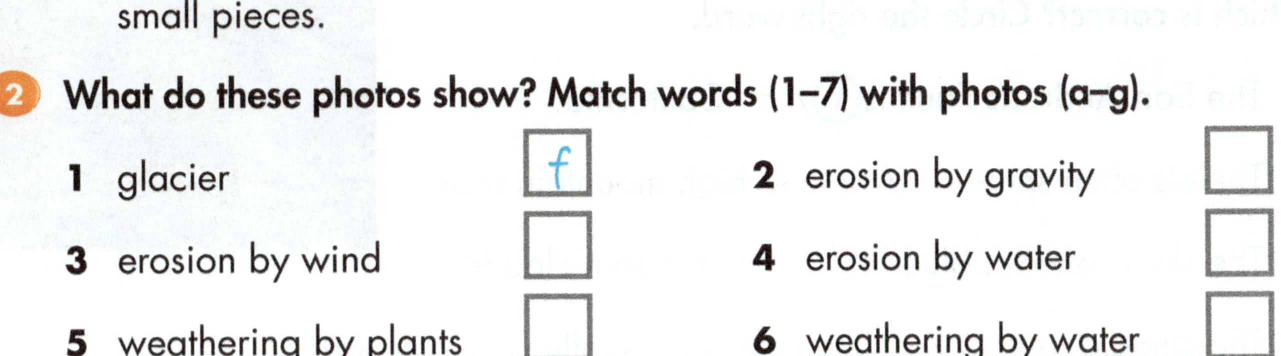

3 How Earth changes. Write the correct word.

1 slow/slowly

The lakes evaporated ____________.

The evaporation was ____________.

2 final/finally

In the ____________ stage, the lava flows down the side of the volcano.

____________, the lava flows down the side of the volcano.

3 constant/constantly

Landforms change ____________. Change is ____________ in this area.

4 Adjective or adverb? Complete with the adjective or adverb form (-ly) of the words in bold.

1 Rivers can ____________ carry large pieces of rock to the sea.　**easy**

2 ____________, the ground started to shake.　**sudden**

3 Weathering can be a very ____________ process.　**slow**

4 When rain comes down very ____________, it can cause floods.　**quick**

5 How can erosion happen by water? Write sentences to describe different ways it can happen.

1 rainwater / carry away / soil / from / farm fields.

Rainwater carries away soil from farm fields.

2 waves / cause / erosion / along / shoreline.

____

3 waves / carry away / sand / from / shoreline.

____

4 during / flood, / rain and floodwater / carry away / sand and mud / from / river banks.

____

Review 4–6

1 What can you remember? Do the quiz. Circle a, b, or c.

1 An ecosystem is ______________.
   a a place that has everything a living thing needs to live
   b the plant life and climate of an environment
   c the living and nonliving parts of an environment that interact together

2 A food chain shows ______________.
   a which animal is the strongest
   b how food is produced
   c the transfer of energy from one living thing to another

3 If you have chickenpox antibodies in your immune system, ______________.
   a you will be protected from getting chickenpox
   b you'll get sick with chickenpox
   c you'll get sick with chickenpox when you're an adult

4 You usually know you are sick because you have ______________.
   a medications
   b allergens
   c symptoms

5 The water that falls to Earth from clouds is called ______________.
   a the water cycle
   b condensation
   c precipitation

6 What causes erosion?
   a The movement of water and air
   b A plant that grows inside a crack in a rock
   c Freezing air

You get one point for each correct answer. What's your score?
1–2 Not good   **3–4** OK   **5–6** Excellent

2 **Which is the odd one out? Circle and explain why it does not belong to the group.**

1 prairie dog   cow   lion   zebra

All the other animals are ________________________________.

2 bacteria   viruses   cells   parasites

All the other things are ________________________________.

3 mushrooms   earthworms   grass   bacteria

All the other things are ________________________________.

4 mountain   valley   ocean   plain   plateau

All the other things are ________________________________.

5 rain forest   coral reef   tunnel   grassland

All the other things are ________________________________.

6 asthma   allergy   flu   diabetes

All the other diseases are ________________________________.

3 **What is it? Write the words. (All of the words are nouns.)**

1 When water becomes vapor ________________

2 It can be viral, bacterial, or fungal. ________________

3 A long period without rain ________________

4 The top layer of Earth ________________

5 Your doctor will give you this medication to fight bacteria. ________________

6 It makes your body produce antibodies to fight a disease. ________________

7 When the ground shakes ________________

8 An ecosystem of the Amazon River ________________

9 It causes soil and rock to go down a slope. ________________

10 An animal that eats only meat ________________

Unit 7 — Earth and Our Universe

How do objects in space affect one another?

1 **What do the different photos show? Write the missing letters.**

1 s p r i n g

2 __ u __ m __ __ __

3 __ __ ll

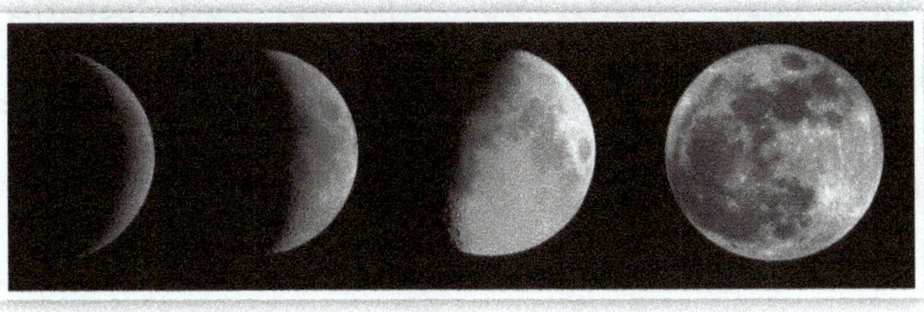

4 w __ __ __ __ e __

5 the ph __ __ s __ __ of the __ oo __

6 __ a __ t __ __ e

7 n __ __ __ __ __ t __ m __

2 **How about you? What season is it now? Which is your favorite season? Compare the daytime and the nighttime. Say what the weather is like.**

We're now in ____.

My favorite season is ____________ because ____________________________.

The daytime is ____.

The weather is ____.

3 **What do you think the text in 4 is about? Complete the sentence.**

This text is about _____________________

____

_____________________.

4 **Earth's best friend. Read the text. Complete with words from the box.**

universe	summer	~~daytime~~	Earth
the sun	phases of the moon	spring	

People often say, "I can't live without my cell phone/the Internet/chocolate," but have you ever thought what it is that we really, really cannot live without? I'll give you an idea. Without it, there's no **(1)** _daytime_, there's only nighttime. It's the only reason seasons exist. Without it, there's no **(2)** ___________ or fall, and there's no winter or **(3)** ___________. Without it, there's no light or heat. Without light, plants and animals cannot grow. Without heat, Earth is only a rock floating in the **(4)** ___________.

Yes, it is the sun. The sun and Earth are best friends, but this won't last forever. Earth has depended on the sun for energy for over 4.6 billion years. Scientists think they have another 7 billion years together before the sun dies.

The sun and the moon look like they are the same size in the sky, but this isn't true. The sun is 400 times larger than the moon. Because the sun is also 400 times further away, they seem to be the same size from **(5)** ___________. Depending on the **(6)** ___________, most of the time the moon shines brightly at night, but not with its own light. Where does the light come from? Can you guess?

The light comes from **(7)** ___________.   (Ryan Hanlon, Grade 5)

Lesson 1 · What are Earth's patterns?

1 **The sun and your shadow. Choose the correct words to complete the text.**

Look at the (1) _position_ of the sun. If you are in the northern half of Earth, turn to look toward the south. From sunrise to noon, the sun moves from your left to the middle of the sky. At noon, it is exactly above your head. From noon to sunset, it moves from the middle of the sky to your (2) ____________.

Find an object and look at its (3) ____________. The position of the shadow (to the left or to the right) will tell you if it is morning or afternoon. The (4) ____________ of the shadow will tell you how early or late it is. A long shadow on the right of the object means that it is early in the morning. A shorter shadow tells you it's late morning. If the shadow is very short, it's (5) ____________. In the same way, a shorter shadow on the left of the object tells you it's early afternoon, and a long shadow on the left of the object tells you it's late afternoon.

One more thing you have to think about is the (6) ____________. In London, for example, in early summer, the sun rises around 5 A.M. and sets around 9 P.M. In winter, the times are around 7 A.M. and 4 P.M.

1 length / place / (position)   **2** left / right / front

3 shadow / axis / length   **4** rotation / length / position

5 midday / late / morning   **6** day / time / season

2 **What's the text in 1 about? Choose the best summary.**

The text is about ____________.

a how to set your watch with the sun

b how to tell time without a clock

c how to tell sunrise from sunset

3 **Looking at clues in photos. Read the texts and complete.**

1

Question: When was the photo taken?

You can see the front of a house. You know that the house faces north.

There's a tree in front of the house. There's a very long shadow on the left side of the tree.

A man is standing on the right side of the photo. He's wearing a coat, a scarf, and gloves.

Answer:

The house faces north, so, when I look at the photo, I'm facing (**1**) _____south_____.

The shadow of the tree is on the (**2**) ___________, so it's the (**3**) ___________.

It's a long (**4**) ___________, so it's (**5**) ___________ in the (**6**) ___________.

The way the man is dressed shows it's (**7**) ___________.

In (**8**) ___________, the sun (**9**) ___________ at about 4 P.M., so the time of day must be between (**10**) ___________ and (**11**) ___________.

2

Question: Where in the world was the photo taken?

You can see people having a picnic at the beach. Some other people are swimming in the ocean.

There's a bright sun, and it seems to be very hot.

A young girl is posing for the photo, holding a sign that says *Happy New Year!*

Answer:

The weather shows that the season is (**1**) ___________.

The sign shows that the date is (**2**) ___________.

The first month of the year in the northern half of Earth is in (**3**) ___________, so we must be in the (**4**) ___________ half of Earth, where it's (**5**) ___________.

The photo was probably taken at a beach in (**6**) ___________ or (**7**) ___________.

4 **Different times. Complete the table with words from the box.**

> sunrise / sunset   (the) spring
> Monday   4.00 P.M. / 10.30 A.M.
> the past / the future   New Year's Day
> May 1st   the afternoon

in + month/year/ season/period of time	*on* + day	*at* + clock time/time of day
in June	on ____________	exception = *in the morning*, etc.
in ____________	on that day	at midday, midnight
in ____________	on ____________	at ____________
in 2015	on ____________	at night
in ____________		at ____________

5 **Talking about time. Complete with *in*, *on*, or *at*.**

1 _On_ June 1st, in London (in the northern half of the planet), sunrise was ______ 4.49 A.M. and sunset was ______ 9.08 P.M. In Sydney (in the southern half of the planet), sunrise was ______ 6.51 A.M. and sunset was ______ 4.54 P.M.

2 It is usually colder ______ the morning than it is ______ the evening. The hottest time of the day is usually early ______ the afternoon.

3 ______ spring and fall, the length of the night and the day are about the same. ______ March 20th and September 22nd, they are exactly the same length.

4 On some calendars, seasons begin ______ the first day of the month and end ______ the last day. For example, summer begins on June 1st and ends ______ August 31st. On other calendars, the seasons start and end on different dates each year. In 2016, summer started ______ June 20th, which was the longest day of the year in the northern hemisphere. It ended ______ September 22nd, when the nighttime and daytime were equal length.

Lesson 2 • What is known about the moon?

1 **What can you see in the photos? Unscramble the words.**

1 hpssea fo het nomo _phases of the moon_

a ewn onom **b** stifr utqrrea **c** lufl noom **d** rtdih rerautq

_____________ _____________ _____________ _____________

2 erctar _____________ **3** ospeeeltc _____________

2 **Describing the phases of the moon. Match.**

1 new moon

a At the end of the second week, all of the lit half of the moon is visible.

2 first quarter

b At the end of the third week, the moon looks like a half circle again.

3 third quarter

c At the end of the first week, the moon looks like a half circle.

4 full moon

d Early in week one, all of the moon appears dark.

3 Which of the facts is correct? Circle a or b.

Moon Facts

1 a Only one side of the moon is lit because the moon produces light on one side only.

b Only one side of the moon is lit because the sun shines on one side only.

2 a The phases of the moon change in a cycle that repeats every 27 days.

b The phases of the moon change in a cycle that repeats every 29 1/2 days.

3 a The moon spins on its axis and revolves around Earth.

b The moon revolves around Earth only.

4 a We see the same side of the moon because it takes the same amount of time to rotate on its axis as it does to move around Earth.

b We see the same side of the moon because, as Earth moves around the sun, the moon travels with it.

4 What is the comparative form of these adjectives? Write.

long — _Longer_

short — ______________

high — ______________

low — ______________

large — ______________

small — ______________

near — ______________

big — ______________

5 Comparing different times. Complete the sentences. Choose an adjective from the box and write it in the comparative form.

near   cold   bright   cool   hot   high

1 In summer, the temperatures are usually ___higher___ than in winter.

2 In spring, the weather is usually ___________ than in summer.

3 The moon is ___________ than Earth at night.

4 The moon is ___________ than Earth during the day.

5 A telescope makes things look ___________ than they are.

6 A full moon is ___________ than a first quarter moon.

6 The moon, Earth, and the sun. Write comparisons, using the comparative form.

1 moon / Earth / large

Earth is larger than the moon.

2 moon / sun / bright

____

3 Earth / sun / small

____

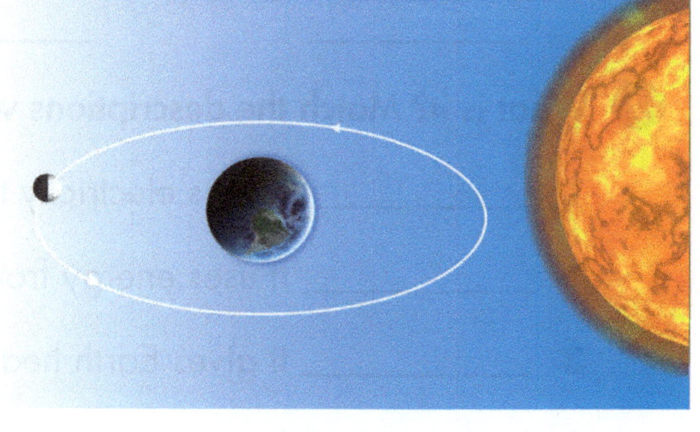

4 full moon / new moon / dark

____

5 sun / moon / hot

____

6 sun / moon / near to Earth

____

Unit 8 — Energy and Its Forms

How can energy change?

1 What can you see in the photos? Unscramble the words.

1 ilhtg ulbb
light bulb

2 crerodre
____

3 nscaeld
____

4 tmsrahnpeo
____

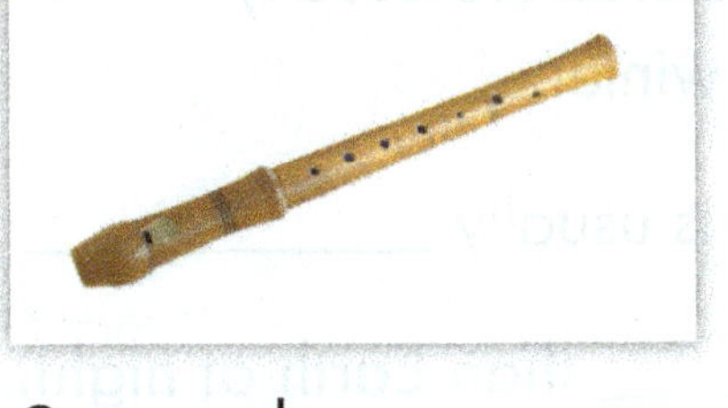

5 oarsl anple
____

6 usn
____

2 What is it? Match the descriptions with words from 1.

1 _light bulb_ It uses electricity to produce light.

2 ___________ It uses energy from the sun to produce electricity.

3 ___________ It gives Earth heat and light.

4 ___________ It uses energy stored in a battery.

5 ___________ It uses air to produce sound.

6 ___________ They burn and produce heat and light.

3 What forms of energy does your family use in your house? Write.

____

4 **Where do these words go? Complete the email with words from the box.**

solar panels   light bulbs   recorder   smartphone   sun   energy

Hi Charlie,

To answer your question, I play baseball every day after school. One day I'd like to play for the Dodgers, one of the greatest baseball teams in the United States! Here's a photo of me in action. My grandpa took it with his **(1)** _smartphone_.

After baseball practice, I go home and have a shower. There's always lots of hot water at home because we have **(2)** ______________ on the roof of our house. We're lucky because where we live the **(3)** ______________ shines most days of the year. My family are still careful about how much **(4)** ______________ we use. We have energy saving **(5)** ______________ in all the lights in every room of the house.

I love music, so, in the evening, after dinner, I usually play the **(6)** ______________. My sisters put on their headphones when I start playing, but I think I sound great! What about you? How do you and your family use energy?

Jake

5 **Finding indirect information in a text. Read 4 again. Answer the questions and say why/how you understand this.**

Reading Tip

There is often indirect information in a text that you can find if you read it carefully.

1 Is baseball important in Jake's life?

Yes, because he plays it every day and wants to be a baseball player.

2 Why does Jake have a shower as soon as he returns home?

____

3 What does this tell you about Jake?

____

4 Why do you think Jake's sisters put on their headphones?

____

Lesson 1 • What are some forms of energy?

1 Which kinds of energy do the photos show? Label with words from the box.

> sound energy   potential/stored energy   kinetic energy
> electrical energy   mechanical energy

1 ______________   2 ______________   3 ______________

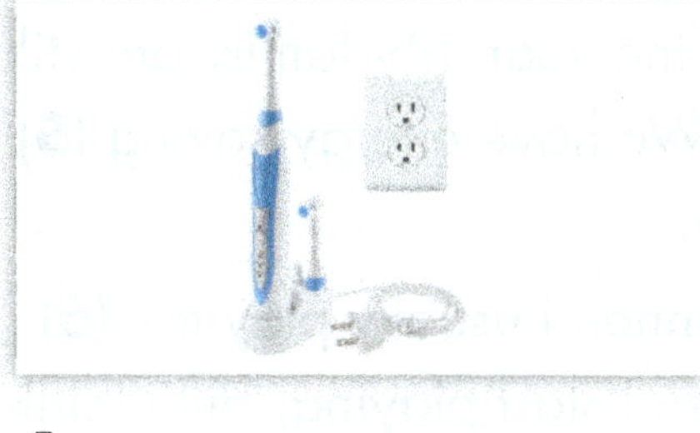 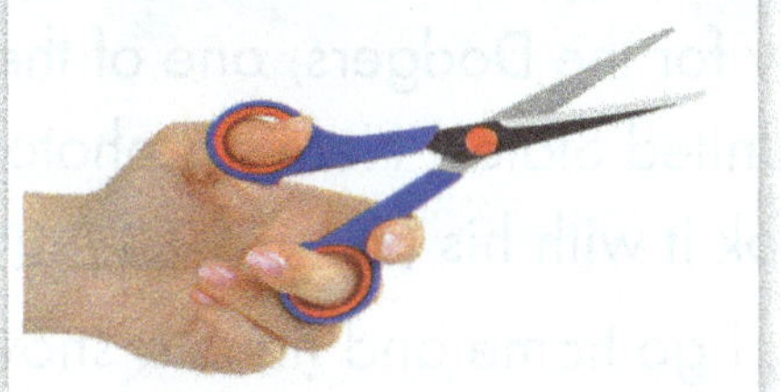

4 ______________   5 ______________

2 What is it? Match the words and the definitions.

1 force   **a** The movement of an object.

2 transfer   **b** A push or pull on an object that causes it to move faster or slower, to stay in one place, or to change shape.

3 motion

    c When a force causes an object to move.

4 work

    d When energy passes from one object to another. For example, kinetic energy passes from a moving object to a still object, and makes it move.

3 Changes in energy. Read, and write sentences to answer the questions.

Dani drives her car to work. On cold days, she turns on the heat to keep warm. She likes listening to music on the car stereo while she drives. What types of energy does she use to do these things?

1 The car engine / turn / gasoline into ?

The car engine turns gasoline into mechanical energy.

2 Electrical energy / be / stored / in the car battery / as ?

3 The car engine / also turn /mechanical energy / into ? to / run the heating system and the stereo.

4 The heating system / of the car / turn / electrical energy / into ?

5 The car stereo / turn / electrical energy / into ?

4 Asking questions about energy. Circle.

1 Who / **What** types of fuel do cars use?

2 **Where** / When does electrical energy come from?

3 **What** / **How** does chemical energy change into kinetic energy?

4 Who / **What** has energy saving machines at home?

5 **What** / **When** does kinetic energy transfer to another object?

6 **How** / **What** happens to an object if a ball hits it?

> **Grammar Tip**
>
> **What** are some forms of energy?
> **Where** does the energy your body uses come from?
> **How** can energy change?

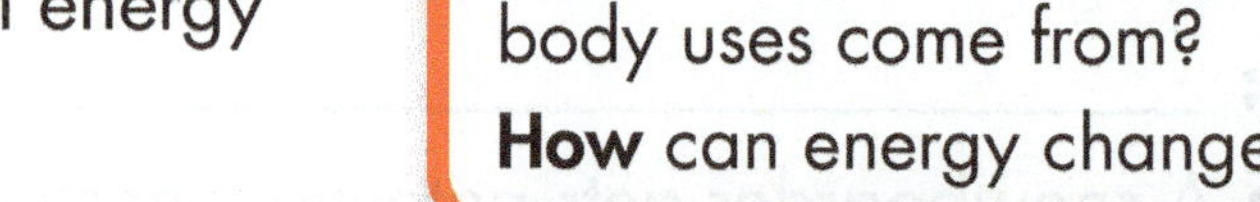

5 **Different kinds of energy. Write to complete the questions.**

1 Q: _____How_____ much oil is there on Earth?

A: There is a limited supply of oil on Earth.

2 Q: _____________ does a solar panel work?

A: It collects energy from the sun.

3 Q: _____________ happens when we turn on a light switch?

A: Electrical energy changes into light energy.

4 Q: _____________ has more potential energy, someone at the top of a hill or someone at the bottom?

A: The person at the top of the hill.

5 Q: _____________ do fossil fuels come from?

A: They come from deep inside Earth.

6 **Asking questions about energy. Write.**

1 Q: _What kind of energy is stored energy?_____________

A: Stored energy is potential energy.

2 Q: ________________________________

A: By replacing all light bulbs with energy saving ones.

3 Q: ________________________________

A: A snowboarder gets potential energy from his high position at the top of the hill.

4 Q: ________________________________

A: A smartphone stops working when its battery has no more energy stored in it.

5 Q: ________________________________

A: A person who is running is using more energy than a person who is walking.

Lesson 2 • What are heat and light energy?

1 **What do the photos show? Complete the sentences with words from the box.**

> burn   warmer   generator   heat   ~~solar panels~~   cooler

1 This spacecraft uses _solar panels_ to make electricity.

2 A ____________ produces electricity.

3 Candles ____________ and produce ____________ and light.

4 They make drinks ____________.

5 It makes the room ____________.

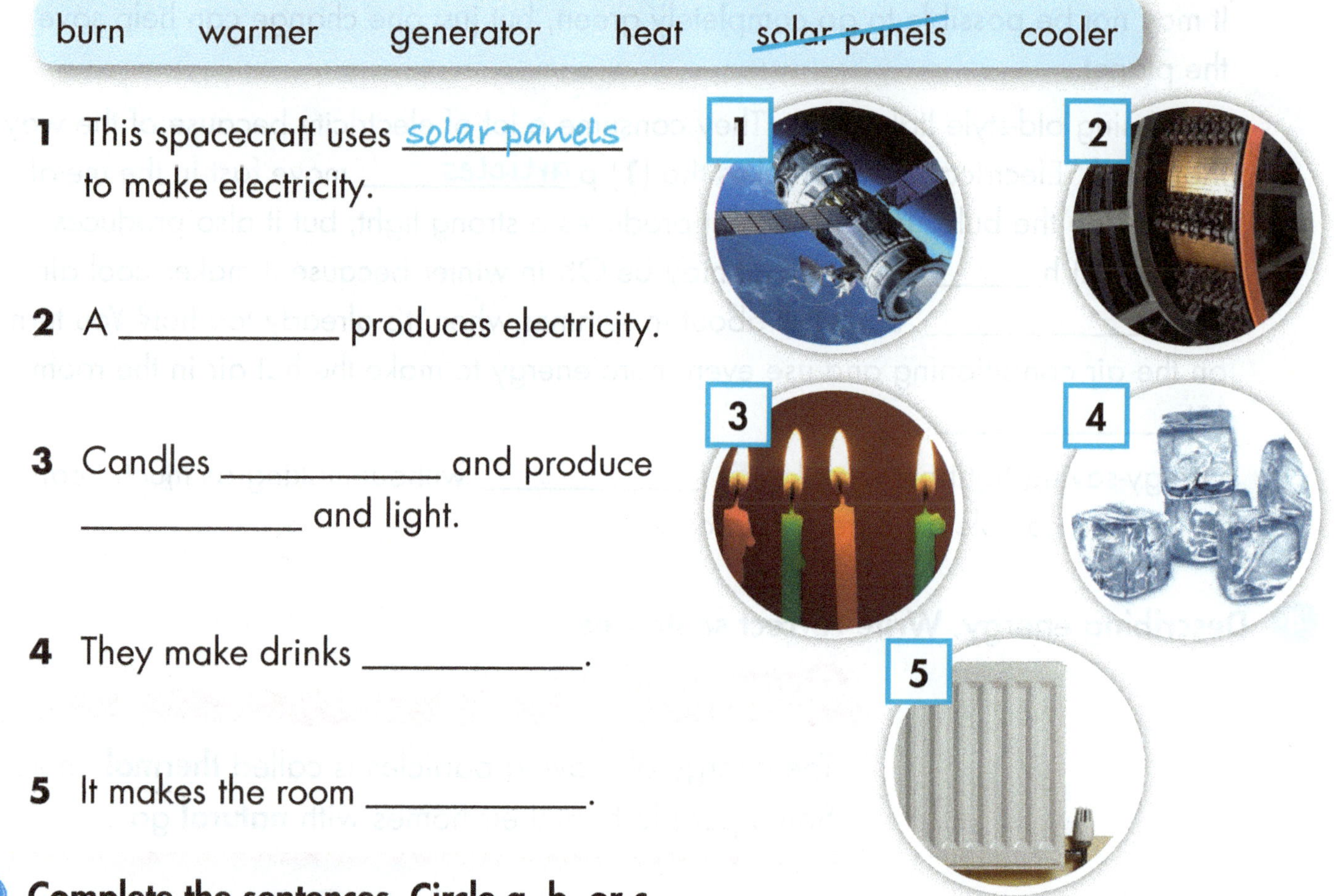

2 **Complete the sentences. Circle a, b, or c.**

1 If we leave an object in the sun, it gets hot because the sun's energy makes
  a the particles inside it stop moving.
  b objects move faster.
  c the particles inside it move faster.

2 Heat travels
  a from warmer to cooler objects.
  b from cooler to warmer objects.
  c only when the environment is hot.

3 When matter burns, it produces energy in the form of
  a particles.
  b heat and light.
  c electricity.

4 A generator is a machine that changes
  a mechanical energy into electricity.
  b electricity into mechanical energy.
  c electrical energy into thermal energy.

3 Saving energy. Complete the text. The first letter of each word is given.

Make ONE Change—SAVE the Planet

It may not be possible to go completely green, but just one change can help save the planet.

Stop using old-style light bulbs. They consume a lot of electricity because of the way they work. Electrical energy makes the **(1)** p_articles___ move fast in the metal wire inside the bulb. This movement produces a strong light, but it also produces a lot of **(2)** h___________. That may be OK in winter because it makes cool air **(3)** w___________, but what about in summer when it's already too hot? You turn on the air conditioning and use even more energy to make the hot air in the room **(4)** c___________.

Energy-saving light bulbs make **(5)** l___________ without making as much heat by using a completely different process.

4 Describing energy. Write correct sentences.

Grammar Tip

The energy of moving particles is called **thermal** energy. Some people heat their homes with **natural** gas.

1 instrument / energy. / A / musical / sound / produces

A musical instrument produces sound energy.

2 kinetic / produces / energy / heat. / of particles / The

____

3 potential / is / energy / energy. / Stored

____

4 use / stored / the / energy / Our bodies / chemical / in food.

____

5 panels / the / energy / Solar / from / collect / sun.

____

5 Talking about energy. Match words from A and B to complete the sentences.

A metal thermal chemical mechanical natural

B energy gas energy object change

1 Burning is a _chemical change_ that can produce light.

2 When you place a _________________ near a heat source, it gets hot very quickly.

3 The _________________ that some lamps produce keeps food warm.

4 One of the fuels we use to heat our homes is _________________.

5 The energy produced when the moving parts of a machine work is _________________.

6 How do these tips save money and energy? Use the prompts to explain.

a Turn off the lights in the rooms you are not using.

Use less electricity → less energy that produces electricity.

You use less electricity so you also use less energy that produces electricity.

b Dry clothes in the sun when possible.

Solar energy → thermal energy. Thermal energy → particles in the water.
Water → evaporates. Clothes → dry. Solar energy → free and renewable.

____

____

____

c Don't keep the windows open when you are heating your home.

Warm air → goes out. Cold air → comes in. More energy → turn cold air into warm air. Less energy → keep air already warm at the same temperature.

____

____

____

Unit 9 Forces and Motion

What forces cause motion?

1 **What can you see in the photos? Add the missing letters to label the photos.**

1 c r a n e **2** m __ __ n __ t **3** __ __ i __ e

4 __ h __ p __ __ n __ __ a __ __ **5** __ o __ __ __ r c __ __ __ __ t e __ **6** __ i __ e

2 **Where can you find them? Match objects from 1 with these places. Write.**

1 playground ____________ **2** supermarket ____________

3 amusement park ____________

3 **What do you use them for? Match objects from 1 with the uses. Write.**

1 picking up and moving very heavy things ____________

2 having fun in the open air ____________

3 picking up light (not heavy) metal things, e.g., paper clips and pins ____________

4 Which objects (machines and tools) do you use every day to help you do things? Write about three of them.

____

____

____

5 Which objects from 1 do these texts describe? Read, and then write the answers.

A _______________

The first rides were popular in Russia in the 16th and 17th centuries, and they didn't have any mechanical parts. They were simple slides made of wood and covered with ice. They were of different heights. Some of them were as high as 20 meters! People went down the slide in wooden boxes or on blocks of ice that moved at great speed. At the end of the ride, there was a big pile of sand.

B _______________

Make sure the wind is right. The best way to find out is to go outside and check. First of all, it has to be a clear day or at least a day without rain clouds. If the force of the wind is enough to move the leaves on a tree, it's a good day for flying. Find a safe area, away from tall trees and electrical power lines.

6 Understanding details in texts. Read the texts in 5 again. Circle the correct answer.

1 In the 16th and 17th centuries, riders used only ___________ energy to move down the ice slide.

   a electrical   **b** magnetic   **c** potential

2 What kind of weather is best for flying a kite?

   a A cloudy day without wind

   b A windy day with no or few clouds

   c A windy, rainy day

Lesson 1 · What is motion?

1 Describing motion. Circle to make correct sentences.

What is motion?

1 The **position** of an object on a map
  a depends on how a person looks at it.
  b is shown in relation to other objects.
  c is not always fixed.

2 The way we describe the position of an object in **motion**
  a is usually in relation to the position and motion of other objects.
  b is always the same.
  c depends on how fast it is moving.

3 **Speed** is
  a the movement of an object.
  b how far an object can go.
  c how fast an object changes its position.

4 An object travels at a **constant speed** when
  a it doesn't change its position.
  b it travels at the same speed.
  c it travels at the same speed as another object.

2 Complete the sentences with the words in bold from exercise **1**.

Photo 1: The brown horse is in ___*motion*___. It's running at a ___________ of 25 kilometers per hour.

Photo 2: The white horse is still. It's ___________ is beside the fence.

Photo 3: In a horse race, a horse does not run at a ___________. If it gets tired, it slows down. When it slows down, the rider makes it go faster again.

3 **Describing position. Look at the photo and write the number of the car.**

1 It's in front of all the other cars. _5_

2 It's behind a red car. There's a green and red car on its left. ____

3 It's got a white car on its right. It's between a green and a red car. ____

4 It's behind all the other cars. ____

5 There's a red car behind it and a white car beside it. ____

4 **Look at the photo. Complete the text with words from the box.**

on the right   in front of   on the left   behind
between   behind   on the left

Hi Jo,

Here's a photo of me and my friends at my birthday party last Saturday. We had a great time! I'm running with a kite I got for my birthday! The boy in the red T-shirt **(1)** _behind_ me, **(2)** _____________, is my best friend, Sam. The three girls **(3)** _____________ side are my neighbors. Leana is wearing an orange T-shirt, and Sue is wearing a dress. Trish is **(4)** _____________ them, a bit farther back. The boys right **(5)** _____________ me (you can't see them very well) are Tom and Nick. My sister is at the back, and the boy **(6)** _____________ her is our cousin Paul (from my mom's side). He's the boy in the purple T-shirt. The girl behind Sam, **(7)** _____________ side of the photo, the one with the long hair and the jeans, is Alex. She's new in my class. She's very pretty, isn't she?

Lesson 2 • How does force affect motion?

1 **What do the words mean? Match to make correct sentences.**

1 **Friction** is a contact force that

2 **Force** is a push or pull on an object that

3 **Magnetism** is a noncontact force that

4 **Iron** is a metal that

5 **Steel** is a hard metal that

6 **Mass** is a measurement that

a shows how much matter there is in an object.

b is made mostly from iron.

c opposes the motion of an object.

d causes it to move, stop, or change direction.

e attracts metal objects containing iron.

f is magnetic. It is found in food and blood.

2 **Can you correct these statements? Write.**

1 **Friction** creates a magnetic field with a north pole and a south pole.

____

2 The south pole of a magnet attracts the **south pole** of another magnet.

____

3 Magnets **attract** wood and plastic.

____

4 Mass has **no effect** on motion because you need **the same** force to push **any** mass.

____

3 **What is a conclusion? What is a fact? Complete the definitions.**

1 A ____________ is something that is known to be true.

2 A ____________ is something that we decide after we have considered all the information.

4 **What do these facts tell us? Read, and complete the conclusions.**

1 **Facts:** John is walking his dog, Flash. When Flash sees a cat, he runs toward it. Flash pulls John with him. John tries to stop Flash, but he cannot, so John runs behind Flash.

Conclusion: John and Flash are pulling in ____opposite____ directions. The ____forces____ John and Flash are applying are not ____________. Flash is pulling with ____________ force than John.

2 **Facts:** John and Flash are walking in the park. Flash sees a man selling hot dogs. He tries to run toward him, but he cannot move. John is pulling Flash's leash and doesn't move, either.

Conclusion: John and Flash are pulling in ____________ directions. The ____________ they are applying are ____________. They are both pulling with ____________ ____________.

Grammar Tip

Magnets work **because** they have a magnetic field around them.
They push with the same force **but** in opposite directions.

5 **Describing force. Join the sentences with *because* or *but*.**

1 The ball goes farther. The player uses more force.
The ball goes farther because the player uses more force.

2 The kite is heavy. The wind is strong and it pulls the kite up.

____

3 Magnets attract metal paper clips. Metal paper clips are made of steel.

____

4 The car moves with difficulty. The road surface produces a lot of friction.

____

Lesson 3 · What is gravity?

1 Which sentence is correct? Circle a or b.

1 **a** Gravity is the force that pulls all objects toward one another.

   b Gravity is the force that makes objects move away from one another.

2 **a** Gravity is a contact force.

   b Gravity is a noncontact force.

3 **a** Gravity pulls everything on Earth's surface toward the center of Earth.

   b Gravity pulls everything on Earth's surface toward the poles of Earth.

4 **a** An object's weight stays the same wherever the object is.

   b An object's weight depends on how close it is to Earth's center.

5 **a** The more matter an object has, the more mass it has, too.

   b Mass has nothing to do with matter.

6 **a** Mass doesn't change when the pull of gravity changes.

   b When weight changes, mass changes, too.

2 Questions about gravity. Complete the answers. Write.

1 **Q:** A skier goes down a mountain at a speed of 130 kilometers per hour. Which force helps him go fast? Which force helps him slow down?

   A: The force that pulls him down, toward Earth, is ____________. The force that helps him slow down is the ____________ between his skis and the ____________.

2 **Q:** If we take an elephant and a mouse to the moon, will they have the same weight as on Earth? Which of the two animals will be heavier?

   A: They will weigh ____________ than on Earth because the moon has ____________ ____________ than Earth, so the pull of gravity is weaker. However, the elephant will still weigh ____________ ____________ the mouse.

3 **Correct the text by adding ' where necessary.**

Two brothers and their uncle are skydiving. The brothers last name is Miller. Their names are James and John. Their uncles name is Adam. Adams last name is Lewis.

- Adams jumpsuit is red.
- The Millers jumpsuits are black.
- James helmet is black.
- Johns helmet is white.

Skydiving is their favorite activity. They like speed and feeling the pull of gravity toward Earths center. Everyone is having a lot of fun!

4 **Work out the puzzle. Use the information in 3 to label the photo.**

5 **Imagine there was no gravity in the classroom. Write what can happen.**

Review 7–9

1 **What can you remember? Do the quiz. Circle a, b, or c.**

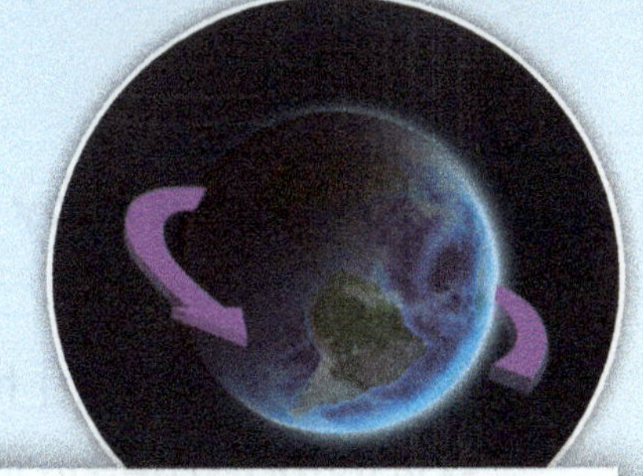

1 When no part of the moon is visible we have a __.
- **a** full moon
- **b** new moon
- **c** half moon

2 Why cannot we see Earth's axis?
- **a** Because it's tilted.
- **b** Because it's deep inside Earth.
- **c** Because it's imaginary.

3 How long does it take Earth to make a complete revolution around the sun?
- **a** 29 days exactly
- **b** 24 hours
- **c** About 365 days

4 A car battery has __.
- **a** kinetic energy
- **b** potential energy
- **c** mechanical energy

5 Spacecraft collect energy in space with the use of __.
- **a** solar panels
- **b** generators
- **c** flywheels

6 Roller coasters travel at a __.
- **a** constant speed
- **b** variable speed
- **c** safety speed

7 Which sentence is true?
- **a** Mass changes to follow changes in gravity.
- **b** The pull of gravity is weaker on objects with more mass.
- **c** Objects with more matter have more mass.

8 Magnetism is a __.
- **a** noncontact force
- **b** contact force
- **c** iron force

You get one point for each correct answer. What's your score?

1–2 Not good   **3–6** OK   **7–8** Excellent

2 **What is it? Write the word.**

1 It makes objects that are far away look nearer and larger. _______________

2 Energy from the sun makes them move faster. _______________

3 It turns kinetic energy into electricity. _______________

4 It attracts anything that has iron in it. _______________

5 It can cause a moving object to slow down or stop. _______________

6 The force that pulls objects toward one another. _______________

7 Most people sleep at this time. _______________

8 When you have light energy, you always have this type of energy, too. _______________

9 A hard metal that has iron in it. _______________

10 The movement of an object. _______________

3 **What are they? Unscramble the letters.**

1 uns = a star

____

2 hpsase = of the moon

____

3 aelncd = it burns and produces light

____

4 rcnae = it lifts heavy objects

____

5 arrect = it's on the surface of the moon

____

6 oncctantno = not touching

____

7 rino = a metal

____

8 artmte = everything is made of it

____

9 orefc = a push or pull

____

10 oratnoti = a complete spin

____

Vocabulary

Units 1–9 · What do I know?

Which words do you want to remember? Write.

Unit 1

Unit 2

Unit 3

Unit 4

Unit 5

Unit 6

Unit 7

Unit 8

Unit 9

I can read and write words about…

		✓	✗
Unit 1	technology and the design process		
Unit 2	plants		
Unit 3	living things		
Unit 4	ecosystems		
Unit 5	body and illness		
Unit 6	earth and weather		
Unit 7	earth and our universe		
Unit 8	energy and its forms		
Unit 9	forces and motion		

Reading Skills

Unit 1   **I can understand the meaning of words I don't know in a text from the words that are around them.**

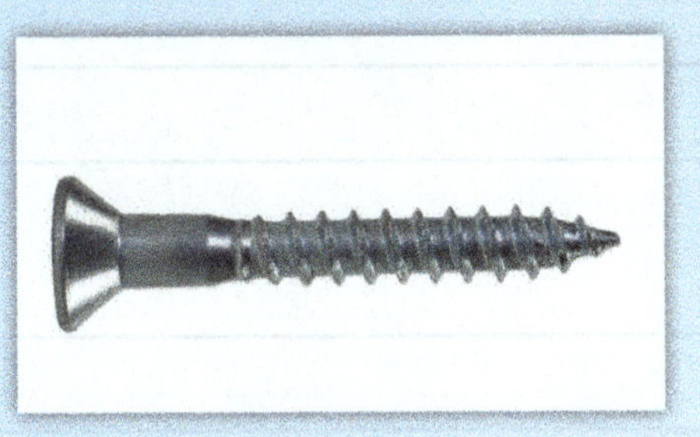

What does the word in bold mean?
A **winding** mountain road is an inclined plane.

Unit 2   **I can predict what kind of information is in a text.**

Read the title below. What kind of information do you think you will find in the text?
From Seed to Flower—Grow Your Own Garden Plants

Unit 3   **I can understand the main idea of a text by underlining the most important words in it.**

Go to page 29 of the Student's Book. Read the text with the title Life Cycles. Underline the most important words in the text.

Unit 4   **I can find information in a text.**

Go to page 42 of the Student's Book. Read the text with the title Parts of an Ecosystem. What type of ecosystem is a marsh?

Units 5–9 · What do I know?

Unit 5   **I can understand where a text comes from by the way it looks.**

Go to page 62 of the Student's Book. Look at the text with the title *Nutrition Facts*. Where does it come from?

Unit 6   **I can make a mind map to organize the information I read in a text.**

Look at pages 71 and 72 of the Student's Book. Make a mind map to help you remember the different types of erosion.

Unit 7   **I can use what I already know about a subject to understand a text better.**

Imagine you are going to read a text about the way Earth moves in space. What do you already know about the ways Earth moves?

Unit 8   **I can understand indirect information from a text.**

Go to page 89 of the Student's Book. Read the text with the title *Energy*. What would happen to the planet if the energy from the sun stopped?

Unit 9   **I can understand the general meaning of a text even when I understand only part of the text.**

Read the extract below. What is it telling you?

The skydiving center is open seven days a week, all year round. It is easy to reach from downtown. If you have questions, drop in and see us at any time between 8 A.M. and 4 P.M.

Writing Skills

Units 1–4 · What do I know?

Unit 1   **Choose and complete.**

lives   complex   machine

I can write about how a complex __________ works and how it has changed people's __________.

I can write about simple and __________ machines.

Unit 2   **Circle the correct words.**

I can write instructions about keeping **animals** / **plants**.

I can **give advice to solve** / **ask questions about** problems that have to do with plants.

Unit 3   **Put the words in the correct order to say what you can do.**

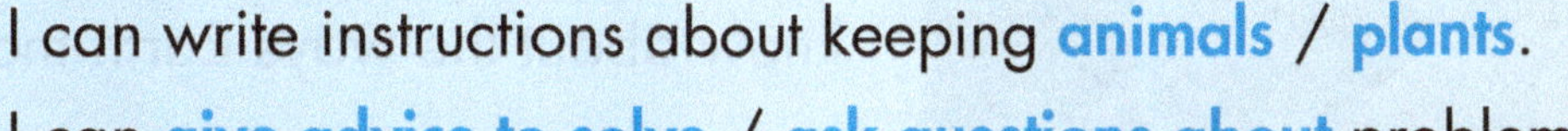

I can write / the / cycle / life / of / about / animals.

____

I can write / animals. / of / descriptions / detailed

____

Unit 4   **Cross out the one thing you cannot do.**

I can write a description of an ecosystem, predict how it will develop in the future, say how the plants and animals that live in it interact, and explain how they have adapted to it.

Units 5–9 · What do I know?

Unit 5 **Circle the correct words.**

I can write about a type of **flu** / **disease**, say what causes it, and describe its **symptoms** / **infection**.

Unit 6 **Choose and complete.**

surface   erosion   changes

I can write about how the ___________ on Earth's ___________ affect people's lives.

I can write about how ___________ by water happens.

Unit 7 **Write the missing word to say what you can do.**

I can write about the seasons, the weather, ___________, and nighttime.

Unit 8 **Put the words in the correct order to say what you can do.**

I can explain which / energy / a / uses. / of / types / car

____

I can write / for / energy. / tips / saving

____

Unit 9 **Draw lines to make sentences.**

I can draw conclusions   situations.

I can write about imaginary   from facts.

Study Skills

Learning vocabulary

- Choose some important and useful new words from every lesson.
- Don't try to learn too many—six to eight words is a good number.
- Look at the words often. You can stick them on the wall next to your bed or another place you often go.
- Test yourself or ask a friend to test you.

Observing

- Find objects in the natural world that interest you.
- Investigate them closely. What do they…look like?…smell like?…sound like? …feel like?
- Look at the objects from different perspectives: from above, from below, from close up, and from far away.
- Look at the objects over time. What changes? When? How? Why do you think they change?
- Record your findings. You can write descriptions, and draw pictures with labels.

Recording and presenting findings

- Create simple tables to record results.
- Explain a sequence using *First…*, *Next…*, *Finally…*.
- Write sentences to describe your observations. Use adjectives (e.g. *yellow, long, soft*). Use comparatives (e.g. *smaller, louder*).
- Create charts to show your results.
- Draw detailed pictures. Write labels with information.